JOHN GUARE

FOUR BABOONS ADORING THE SUN
AND OTHER PLAYS

John Guare's *Six Degrees of Separation* won the 1990 New York Drama Critics Circle Award for Best Play, as well as the Hull Warriner Award and the Obie. *The House of Blue Leaves* won the New York Drama Critics Circle Award for Best American Play of 1971 and received four Tony awards in its revival at Lincoln Center in 1986. His screenplay for Louis Malle's *Atlantic City* won the New York, Los Angeles, and National Film Critics Circle awards, as well as an Oscar nomination. Mr. Guare, a longtime council member of the Dramatists Guild, was elected in 1989 to the American Academy and Institute of Arts and Letters. He lives in New York.

FOUR BABOONS ADORING THE SUN

▲ ▲ ▲ ▲

AND OTHER PLAYS

JOHN GUARE

VINTAGE BOOKS
A DIVISION OF RANDOM HOUSE, INC.
NEW YORK

CONTENTS

▲ ▲ ▲ ▲

PREFACE

BY SIR PETER HALL

Four Baboons Adoring the Sun was one of the richest experiences I have had in forty years of directing plays, operas, and films. Why? Quite simply, because John Guare was its author. He is a writer of courage, and his desire to create a piece with myth, memory, and present action—all expressed simultaneously—was instantly appealing.

Four Baboons landed on my desk in London in October 1991. I was immediately intrigued by its technical ambitions. I liked choric work from my experience with Greek plays; and I liked mixing music with words from the experience of innumerable opera productions. Even more, I was attracted by the theme that the play was expressing—equating being in love with the fresh eyes and fresh responses of childhood. That is why we all like to be near people in love; and why we all yearn to be in love ourselves. The world seems new.

What also attracted me to *Four Baboons* was that it was a piece of musical theater whose leading players never realized that a musical was happening around them. I have always admired John Guare's work, *House of Blue Leaves* and *Six Degrees of Separation* particularly. He uses the theater boldly and in a thoroughly post-naturalistic way. His plays, with their combination of direct audience address, sudden time shifts, and vivid metaphorical emblems, rely on the sensibility of an age conditioned by the jump cuts and dissolves of the cinema. Yet his work is quintessentially of the theater: he spins his audience's emotions on a quarter. The rich dramatic texture he creates is at its most colorful on the stage: he needs a live audience to make it work.

I telephoned John as soon as I had finished reading the first draft. I wanted to be sure that the play I had responded to was the play he wanted me to direct. He jumped on a plane and we sat for three days in London, meticulously discussing every page. We found that our aims coincided and that our hopes agreed.

In some respects, *Four Baboons* is a masque. Its story—the hesitant meeting of two tribes of young children from previous marriages—is realistic and funny enough. But it uses that reality to climb into regions of emblematic theater that go far above naturalism.

John's vision could only be fulfilled by using the full armory of theatrical techniques: direct audience address in which the actor narrates his past and yet lives it at the same time; choric speaking by the chorus of children, not only to maintain their tempo and inflections, but to emphasize their nature as a group rather than as individuals; and above all music, expressing, in more than twenty short songs, the mythical world through the mouth of the god Eros.

John Guare has a long relationship with the musical theater, going back beyond his Broadway version of *The Two Gentlemen of Verona*. He is a canny dramatist who knows that music can always raise the temperature quicker than words. But unless the writer is very careful, there is a price to pay: simplification. In *Four Baboons,* he was concerned to integrate the two, and to be sure that the music was never decoration.

Four Baboons could be conceived of as a high comedy about people who thought that the enormity of their love could let them make a Faustian bargain with the universe—their love gave them carte blanche. But Guare had set this comic world of high optimism and easy solutions into a dark world of chaotic life forces. These were represented by Eros, and he would be the only singer. Music would therefore play the roles of passion and chaos. And finally, it would produce reconciliation.

But what kind of music? I proposed Stephen Edwards—a

young English composer who had worked with me at the National Theatre, on the Broadway production of *Orpheus Descending,* and on several television films. Edwards and a brilliant sound designer, Paul Arditti, had devised a way of taking natural sound—wind, rain, storms, the sea—and finding and changing the pitch in these sounds. I wanted to produce the feeling of not listening simply to music, but of nature run amok.

Now the piece had to *look* as it was beginning to sound. Tony Walton created the play's mythical world with volcanoes, earthquakes, and visions as its daily bread. He used the angled disc jutting out into the audience that has become the trademark of the Beaumont style. He has made it one of the most imaginative theatrical spaces in the world. On this occasion, he covered it with mosaic and tons of sand to represent the archeological site which was the prime setting of the play. It would split open during an earthquake. Behind it shone an enormous golden disc blazing like the Sicilian sun, which would then turn to reveal a vision of a deer drinking from a waterfall. It then transformed into the face of a perilous cliff the children would scale, and then revolved gently as one of the children fell to a death in Eros' arms and then descended on into the underworld. At the end, the sun would split open to reveal the heart of the flaming volcano. All this looked like the music and the music sounded like the set. And it happened in conjunction with Richard Pilbrow's lights, which held everything together. Bernard Gersten and André Bishop as producers gave us support and enthusiasm that was exemplary.

The play was truly an attempt to write a modern Greek tragedy combining all the instruments of the theater. For me, it succeeded triumphantly. In one hour and twenty minutes, the audience was taken on a long and surprising journey which both moved and excited them. They heard modern wisecracks; strong emotional dialogues; modern American children speaking in rhythmic order and yet sounding completely natural; and short, concentrated songs that reminded them that human in-

stinct was as old as time. They also saw a stage which asked for
their imagination. They saw much more than the literal screen
could have given them.

Weeks after the play closed, John called me in London to tell
me of a woman who had come up to him in the street. She said,
"You wrote that play!" He backed off, as writers do. "No, listen
to me." She told him that *Four Baboons* had allowed her to face
up to her deepest secret shame and finally speak about her
obsession with, and fantasies about, her son's sexuality. The play
had named her secret and freed her. John asked how old her son
was. "Three years old," she said.

The age is immaterial. We are born sexual creatures in the
thrall of Eros, who always lies in wait to awaken us, destroy us,
and renew us. But the play, our work, had invaded her dreams.
And that, after all, had been the challenge: to make a piece of
musical theater out of this collision of a recognizable comic
world and the world of chaotic dreams.

Four Baboons demonstrated the uniqueness of theater and its
ability to invade our dreams. This is why theater remains indis-
pensable. I learned much from this production which I know I
can draw on again and again in the future. I believe we all did.

FOUR BABOONS ADORING THE SUN
AND OTHER PLAYS

FOUR BABOONS
ADORING THE SUN

▲ ▲ ▲ ▲

FOUR BABOONS ADORING THE SUN was originally produced by Lincoln Center Theater in New York City under the direction of André Bishop and Bernard Gersten and began performances on March 18, 1992, at the Vivian Beaumont Theater, with the following cast:

EROS	Eugene Perry
PENNY MCKENZIE	Stockard Channing
PHILIP MCKENZIE	James Naughton
WAYNE	Wil Horneff
LYLE	Michael Shulman
SARAH	Ellen Hamilton Latzen
TEDDY	Alex Sobol
HALCY	Angela Goethals
JANE	Zoë Taleporos
PETER	John Ross
ROBIN	Kimberly Jean Brown
ROGER	Zachary Phillip Solomon

Directed by Sir Peter Hall; music composed by Stephen Edwards; sets by Tony Walton; costumes by Willa Kim; lighting by Richard Pilbrow; sound design by Paul Arditti.

TIME: A summer in Sicily, a few years ago.

▲ ▲ ▲ ▲

Primitive and ancient sounds.
The austere marble wreckage of Classical times.
EROS *rises out of the smoking primordial ooze.*
He carries a golden disc.

EROS: The start of another perfect day
                Something will go wrong
(*He reflects light from the disc into the audience.*)
                    I do not control things
                    I simply urge them along

                    My name is not important
                    But be that as it may
                    I was born of a fling
                    The night had with the day

                    All right, my name is Eros.
(*It reverberates around the theater:*) Eros Eros Eros
                    That's E.R.O.S.
                    And who it is I'm waiting for
(*He shines the disc around the audience catching their faces.*)
                    Is anybody's guess.

                    Is it you
                    Or you
                    Or

(PHILIP *and* PENNY MCKENZIE, *early 40s, khaki work clothes, tanned,*
hard working, run down the stairs.)

PENNY: Are we late?

PHILIP: Where do we go? Down this way? Or that way?

(EROS *catches them in his light.*
They freeze.)

EROS: Two lovers in an airport
         I wonder what they'll do?

(*A great neon sign "Alitalia" flashes on.*
The sounds turn into an airport.
PENNY *and* PHILIP *run on.*
They look up at various screens.)

PENNY: Is that us?

PHILIP: They talk so fast.

PENNY: At least they're not on strike.

ANNOUNCEMENT: Arrival JFK-Milano-Palermo

PHILIP: Listen—Milano—is that the flight? Listen—JFK-Milano-
    Palermo—

EROS: The plane from America
         The plane from America
         The plane from America has now arrived!

PHILIP: There it is. On time. On schedule! The kids are here!

EROS: The plane from America has now arrived.

PENNY: My God! The plane's on time! We're on time! That is
    a miracle!

PHILIP: A miracle? Penny, we just left the dig early.

PENNY: It *is* a miracle. Before you and I got together, I would
    have arrived, running through this airport screaming like a
    banshee, late because every road in the world was under
    construction, every traffic light was red, everything strikable
    was on strike. But you and I fall in love. Construction on
    every road finishes. Nothing's ever on strike. Every traffic

light is always green. We find a parking space. And planes arrive on time. Don't tell me that's not a miracle.

(*They kiss. Deep. Passionate.*)

PHILIP: Penny, see that baggage carousel? Let's you and I hop on that shiny silver circle— Come on, what do you say?

PENNY: It'd be the only place we haven't made love.

PHILIP: and we'll spin there for eternity, revolving around and around.

PENNY: What's wrong?

PHILIP: Wayne. What if Wayne hasn't forgiven me yet? Oh Christ, that last time I saw Wayne. I went to say goodbye to everybody and there's my son crouched up in my packed suitcase, polishing off a quart of cheap bourbon. This glare of dazed hatred in his eyes. I swatted him. Yes. I hit him. To see a *child* in a suitcase drinking.

PENNY: Philip! That was not you. That was his life. That was home. My little Halcy took ballet lessons for a year. When *The Nutcracker* was over I found this silver tinfoil wad of pot in her room. I said, Halcy, it can't always be *Nutcracker* time. She said, Mom, if I stop dancing I have to listen to you and Daddy fight. She blew smoke right in my face. You and I have saved her from that. You and I are saving every one of our kids.

PHILIP: Jesus, I love you, Penny.

PENNY: They won't be ordinary kids. They'll be kids who lived in Sicily

PHILIP: who were archaeologists

PENNY: who worked with their parents in the field side by side. Our kids are an unexplored dig. We don't want to lose anything of value in them. That's our greatest task. It's going to work! Philip! *We've* done it! Now the kids are about to escape the twentieth century!

PHILIP: Yes! Lucky kids! Look at me, Penny. Four Baboons Adoring the Sun. Remember those baboons—

PENNY: Four Baboons Adoring the Sun.

(*They make a palms-up gesture.*)

PHILIP: Strong.

PENNY: Strong. Yes. Four Bab—

PHILIP: Wait—announcement—

PHILIP: That's it! The plane's landed. They're safe! They're here!

(EROS *assumes the identity of Passport Control.*
THE CHILDREN *enter one by one.*

They each present their passport to EROS *and run happily to the center of the stage and freeze in place.*)

EROS:	Wayne	
	Sarah	Benvenuto a Sicilia
	Lyle	Benvenuto
	Teddy	
	Halcy	Benvenuto a Sicilia
	Jane	Benvenuto a Sicilia
	Peter	
	Robin	Benvenuto
	Roger	Benvenuto a Sicilia

(*Everyone is frozen in place in joy for a moment.*
PHILIP'S KIDS—WAYNE, *age 13;* SARAH, *age 11;* LYLE, *age 10;* TEDDY, *age 7—are dressed very casually: jogging, surfing, jams.*
PENNY'S KIDS—HALCY, *age 13;* JANE, *age 11;* PETER, *age 9;* ROBIN *and* ROGER, *age 7—travel in blazers and gray flannels.*
Then they break and scream with joy and run to their parents.)

PENNY: Oh my arms and legs and eyes and ears and soul.

PHILIP: You're all big and wonderful and healthy. Kiss me. Let me smell you. You beauties.

PENNY: Oh kids, it's been ten weeks. Ten weeks!

(*Everyone embraces.*
Then PENNY *and* PHILIP *detach themselves and stand between the two groups of* KIDS.)

PENNY: Kids. You remember Philip.

PHILIP: Kids. This is Penny.

PENNY: How wonderful to meet you!

PHILIP: Wayne. Teddy. Sarah. Lyle.

PENNY: Halcy. Jane. Peter. Robin. Roger.

(THE KIDS *size each other up.*
They turn on rival ghetto blasters of rock.
Cacophony.)

PENNY: I don't think the music is—

(PENNY *and* PHILIP *switch off the radios.*
Silence.)

PHILIP: Didn't you all get to be friends on the plane?

LYLE: (*Speaking in meter*) Mommy told us to give you a letter.
[Note: Throughout the play, except for Wayne and Halcy, the children speak in strict meter. *E.g.*, "Mómmy tóld us to gíve you a létter."]

WAYNE: Yes. A letter from Mom.

(WAYNE *hands a letter to* PHILIP.
THE KIDS *speak metrically.*)

HALCY: We flew over a volcano.

PENNY: Mount Etna!

SARAH: This island has a volcano!?

PHILIP: We can drive up there this afternoon!

ROBIN: A volcano?

TEDDY: A volcano!

PETER: We should've been told about a volcano

JANE: before we agreed to come

ROBIN: I'm calling Daddy

JANE: I'm calling

ROGER: *I'm* calling

PENNY'S KIDS: Daddy! Daddy! Daddy!

PENNY: Darling, it's a lovely volcano. Lava comes from the word *lover*. Don't be afraid of any volcanoes. Now does everybody have their bags? I'm sure your father knows Sicily contains Mount Etna.

PHILIP: We can drive up there right now.

PENNY: I am *saving* the volcano. When we have succeeded in becoming a family, when we are forged together, when we have done what we are setting out to do, *then* we shall *all* drive up to Mount Etna. Lava streaming through the night, all orange.

PHILIP: Etna's back that way.

PENNY: Etna can be anywhere I want it to be. Got your bags! Let's go to the car—

(*They walk out of the airport.*)

PHILIP: *Lover* from *lava*? Where'd you pull that out of—

PENNY: Don't ask—

(*They step out into blinding Sicilian sun.*)

PENNY: Where's the car?

PHILIP: Where's the car?

PENNY: We've lost the car.

PHILIP (*calling off*): Dove e l'auto?

(PHILIP *goes off.*)

JANE: Daddy's very happy and didn't send you best greetings or anything.

PETER: You know Daddy's secretary?

JANE: Daddy's secretary sleeps in your bed.

(PENNY *suddenly snaps.*)

PENNY: Did your father tell you to say that!

JANE: No!

PETER: No!

(PENNY *recovers.*)

PENNY: Hurray for Daddy!

(PENNY *turns out to us as if she is in a later time—say, three years hence—relating a story to us, a story she is still puzzling over.*)

Mel had what he wanted. I had what I wanted. Everybody had what they wanted. Their father was a congressman. My leaving had actually helped Mel get reelected. He got the sympathy vote. Mel had found his true constituency. The embittered male.

(*To* THE KIDS.)

Look me right in the eye. I. Love. You. All. Pull it together, Roger. Breathe in deep! You're here!

SARAH: This is Sicily?

JANE: This is Sicily?

PENNY: Yes! This is indeed Sicily.

(PHILIP *returns*.)

PHILIP: Where's the car?

LYLE: I told the kids at school we were coming to the pyramids.

PHILIP: That's Egypt. The car has to be over here—

SARAH: Where's the pyramids?

ROGER: I thought this was archaeology.

PENNY: It is. You parked down here—

LYLE: Where's the temples?

HALCY: You don't know where the car is?

LYLE: You lost the car?

JANE: Where did you put the car?

SARAH: Daddy! You're an A-hole!

PHILIP: Sarah! That's your mother talking!

SARAH: I want to know where the car is!

PETER: Tell me where the car is!

ROBIN: Where's my car?

ROGER: We lost my car?

TEDDY: I want our car!

PENNY: I'll find the car—

(PENNY *goes off to find the car.*
All THE KIDS, *except* WAYNE, *exclaim noisily. Then:*)

WAYNE: Kids! Be quiet! That means all of you. It's a new country. Dad's excited to see us. Give Dad a chance. He'll find
the stupid car. Doesn't he always find the car?

(THE KIDS *are quiet*.)

PHILIP: Wayne. Grazie.

WAYNE: Dad? Who was the Duke of Windsor?

PHILIP: I give you Sicily and you give me the Duke of Windsor?

WAYNE: Mom said you threw away an empire. Like the Duke of Windsor.

PHILIP: The archaeology department at the University of Cal San Luis Obispo hardly rates as an empire.

WAYNE: But who's the Duke of Windsor?

(PENNY *returns from another direction*.)

PENNY: He gave up the throne of England for the woman he loved.

WAYNE: Was he a hero? Were they very beautiful?

HALCY: I saw a TV movie about the Duke and Duchess of Windsor. They were very beautiful.

PENNY: TV docudramas have a very slender relation with the truth.

WAYNE: Threw away an empire?

HALCY: Yes!

(HALCY *gives* WAYNE *a high-five handshake*.)

WAYNE: I like that, Dad.

(WAYNE *laughs and gives* HALCY *a high-five handshake*.)

PENNY: I found the car. Now we have a long car ride! Halcy, you take the girls to the little girls'—

PHILIP: Wayne—the boys follow Wayne.

(THE KIDS *go.*
PHILIP *and* PENNY *turn to us, three years hence.*)

PENNY (*to us*): The kids went to the bathroom. I wanted to shoot myself. I just wish I hadn't blown up at my kids. But what had happened to the boy who so worried Philip? Wayne. Wayne was thirteen years old and on the brink of everything. Wayne was supportive. Wayne was—enchanting.

PHILIP (*to us*): I have to tell you—I was dreading Wayne's arrival. But he was a different boy from that kid I last saw in my suitcase. He was sweet. He was loving. Why had he changed? As usual, I could have killed their mother. Fourteen pages of scrawled hatred detailing how various parts of my anatomy should be nailed onto certain archaeological sites—

(*Play returns to present.*
PHILIP *crumples up Jeanne's letter in a rage.*)

PENNY: What was in Jeanne's letter?

PHILIP (*bright*): Oh, nothing. Sarah's a vegetarian. Teddy's allergic to walnut oil. Jeanne sends her love.

PENNY: Walnut oil? If that's the least of our problems. I'm crazy about your kids. Photos don't do anybody justice—but your kids—Knockouts!

PHILIP: Your kids! Beauties! Isn't Wayne something?

PENNY: And Sarah! I hate to say it. My favorite! She's so damaged. I'm going to give her the love her mother couldn't. God! The kids are here! I feel complete!

(*She takes a swig of water from her bag.*)

PHILIP: Do you know how smart my kids are?

PENNY: Do you know how smart my kids are?

PHILIP: Off the charts—

PENNY: My kids don't even have charts. Are we going to make it?

PHILIP: We are!

PENNY: How do we accomplish that miracle?

PHILIP: What's the one rule of Sicily?

PENNY: What?

PHILIP: Omertà.

PENNY: Omertà?

PHILIP: Never reveal what you're feeling.

PENNY: Omertà. What are they doing in that bathroom?

PHILIP: Laughing at us.

PENNY: I don't want them laughing at us. I want them to see the value of what we're doing. We don't have any pyramids. We have beads. Pots. I want them to be thrilled by Sicily. I want them to see Sicily through our eyes. To see its grandeur—its majesty.

(THE KIDS *return*.)

HALCY: That toilet's filthy!

TEDDY: There was no soap.

LYLE: There's no paper!

JANE: Sarah threw up in the toilet.

SARAH: I did not throw up in the toilet!

ROGER: It stinks in there.

PETER: I feel sick.

ROBIN: And I hate Sicily!

PHILIP: We set?

PENNY: Everybody listen up. Before we get in the van—

PHILIP: What are you doing?

PENNY: I am so sick of my name. Penny. What kind of a name is Penny? And Philip—what kind of name is Philip?

PHILIP: It's not much, but it's my name. What do you mean?

(PENNY *takes two clear plastic sacks filled with slips of paper out of her shoulder bag and hands them out to* THE KIDS.)

PENNY: I've written down names and you can each draw a name out of the bag and that will become your new Sicilian name and we will find out everything we can about your new name. Girls draw from the girl bag. Boys draw from the boy bag. Roger, you draw from the boy bag.

(*Each* KID *reaches in and picks a slip of paper.*)

EROS: Attenzione Prego
          Arethusa
          Daedalus
          Aphrodite
          Adonis
          Pallas Athena
          Prometheus
          Apollo
          Artemis
          Icarus

WAYNE: I'm Icarus.

(PENNY *produces a thick book out of her shoulder bag.*)

PENNY: Now we can look up who that is.

(PENNY *finds the right page and passes the book to* WAYNE.)

WAYNE (*reads*): Icarus is a boy—

PENNY: Say *I*. This is you. *I* am a boy who—

(*As* WAYNE *reads, the sound of rushing wings.*)

WAYNE: was trapped in a labyrinth and his father, Daedalus

LYLE: I'm Daedalus!

PHILIP: No! I'm his father. That makes me Daedalus!

WAYNE: invented flying.

EROS: Icarus
             Sits on a beach
             Icarus
             Looks up at those cliffs, those cliffs
             Icarus
             Dreams, dreams of flight. Dreams of Flight!
             Dreams of Flight.
             Dreams of Flying!

WAYNE: Dreams of flying. Oh, I like that! Icarus! Thank you, Daedalus.

(HALCY *takes* PENNY's *book.*)

HALCY: But it says here the sun melted his wings and Icarus crashed into the sea and died. Every one of these stories ends horribly. People turn into trees. Girls turn into spiders. Dogs eat people. What's wrong with these stories?

PENNY: Let's get in the car.

LYLE (*to* PENNY): Why didn't you pick?

PHILIP: Penny already has a mythical name. Penelope. The faithful wife who waited and waited and waited and waited for her husband to come home. That's who Penny is.

JANE: She didn't wait for Daddy.

ROGER: She left Daddy.

JANE: Yeah! She left Daddy.

ROBIN: Yeah! She left Daddy.

PETER, JANE, ROBIN, ROGER: Yeah! She left Daddy.

PHILIP: She waited for me. That makes me Odysseus. My travels are over. I'm finally home. See! There's a happy ending!

PENNY: Get in the car, Artemis! Do you have your bag, Adonis? Andiamo! Andiamo! Vite! Vite!

PHILIP: You haven't been here an hour and you already have new names.

PENNY: The Duke of Windsor? Good God.

PHILIP: My good Duchess?

PENNY: Everything bellezza, my excellent Duke.

(*The bags piled up become the van.*
PHILIP *and* PENNY *happily step into the van,* THE CHILDREN *following.*)

WAYNE: My good Duchess. I like that. My good Duchess.

HALCY: My excellent Duke.

(WAYNE *and* HALCY *smile at each other and bow and step into the van.*)

PHILIP: This is your captain speaking. Extinguish smoking material and fasten your seat belts.

PENNY (*reading the road signs*): Curva pericolosa—dangerous curve (*They swerve to the left.*) Svolta stretta—sharp turn (*They swerve to the right.*)

PHILIP: Dosso—bump
(*They bump.*)
Everything started here. This is where the gods came on holiday. Don't look at the petrochemical plants—

SARAH: I hate these highways

LYLE: It looks like home

JANE: It looks like the Connecticut turnpike

ROBIN AND ROGER: Yeah, the Connecticut turnpike!

TEDDY: This is California

SARAH: I thought Sicily was different

PETER: You said Sicily was beautiful

JANE: You said Sicily was wonderful

PHILIP: Let's get off this highway.

PENNY: I've got a map.

EROS: Turn off the road!
         Take the next exit
         Now turn left
         Take the second right
         I do not control
         I offer a choice
         I say to your soul
         Rejoice
         Do you hear the sea?
         The road is dirt
         Get lost for a moment
         But remember this route

PHILIP: Already I miss this place. Kids! This is the real Sicily!
    Look at it! Smell the sea! See the poppies!

PENNY: I cannot wait to come here again! Remember this road!
    It's—

EROS: —gorgioso!

PENNY: gorgioso! Now those poppies are red because Aphrodite
    set her dogs on Adonis and the dogs ripped poor Adonis to
    shreds and the blood made all the flowers red—

THE KIDS: Yuk.

HALCY: Another disgusting story.

PENNY: Oh well, it's not important how the poppies got red—

PHILIP: Nothing will happen to you—

PENNY: Should we even be on this road? Is this even a road—
    Look!

(EROS *sets up a cafe.*)

EROS: You must always stop at a cafe by the sea
         You must bask in the sun by this lunatic, crazily blue
             sea.
         You must watch your kids play
         The eternal game of Ringalevio!
         Ringalevio!
         See them running in and out of the water
         See them throwing an orange Frisbee
         All the while you drink Bellinis!
         What are Bellinis?
         Champagne and fresh white peaches!

(EROS *serves cool drinks to* PENNY *and* PHILIP *as they watch their*
CHILDREN *in the distance.*)

PHILIP: Look at them throw that ball. Higher! Higher!

PENNY: Don't swim out too far! That's right. Not too rough!

PHILIP: Listen! "Ollie ollie oxen free."

PENNY: "Ollie ollie oxen free"—haven't heard that in years—

PHILIP: "Home free!" Yes! Everybody's home free—

PENNY: Look! They run around in one great blur!

PHILIP: They *like* each other!

PENNY: They get along! Thank you, gods!

(EROS *bows.*)

PHILIP: Can't tell who's yours.

PENNY: Can't tell who's mine.

(*And then a sound—the wind?—the sea?—tremolo—a warning.*
PENNY *and* PHILIP *turn to us, three years hence.*)

PENNY (*to us*): I heard the murmuring first. It wasn't a babble
like a babbling brook. But it had the quality of clear water
running over glittery stones.

PHILIP: Can't tell who's yours. Can't tell who's mine—it's all
going to be fine—(*to us.*) But then I heard it too—I heard—
what?—the sound of exotic birds clawing the earth—

(*Play returns to present.* WAYNE *and* HALCY *appear.*)

WAYNE: "Is there a moment when all our lives are touched by
grace and we discover our true selves?"

HALCY: "I don't dare."

WAYNE: "We have to dare."

HALCY: "I've got to get home."

WAYNE: "We've been given a gift."

HALCY: "I just came into town to have lunch. Things like this
don't happen. Not to me."

WAYNE: "Not to me."

HALCY: "I hate my life."

WAYNE: "I hate my life. I can't go on."

HALCY: "I'll die if I don't make a change and have love in my
life."

WAYNE: "I'll die."

HALCY: "I'll die."

WAYNE: "I'll die."

(*They disappear.*
Three years hence.)

PHILIP (*to us*): The breeze changed direction.

PENNY (*to us*): I asked myself if I was hearing contents of letters
we had written to each other.

PHILIP (*to us*): I asked myself if I was hearing fragments of phone
calls we made late at night while we were working all this
out.

PENNY (*to us*): They couldn't have been eavesdropping on the
phone.

PHILIP (*to us*): They couldn't have been reading our mail.

PENNY AND PHILIP (*to us*): Could they?

EROS: Are you hallucinating?

(*Play returns to present.*)

PENNY: These Bellinis.

PHILIP (*laughs*): I thought I heard . . .

PENNY (*bright laugh*): I thought *I* heard . . .

PHILIP: You don't want to know what I thought I heard. No
more Bellinis!

(EROS *clears the Bellinis.*)

PENNY: Tell me everything is going to be okay.

PHILIP: Tell the gods. They're all around us.

EROS: Tell me
             I'm here

PENNY: Gods! Make them have a happier life than we've had.

PHILIP: Till now! Don't forget till now.
        Okay, kids! Back in the van!

PENNY: Can we get it all together?

PHILIP: But we have. That's what you better get used to. We're living in a new universe. You're used to living in Universe A.

PENNY: Universe A?

PHILIP: Adults—us—are over here in Universe A. All facts and reasons and explanations. Every aspect of life dragged down with the same old same old. But over here—please step forward and examine shiny, buoyant Universe B. The kids' universe. Now it's yours. It's where we are.

EROS: Have you found a moment
          You think you're gifted
          To see the present
          Annihilate the past?

PENNY: I have no interest in childhood.

PHILIP: It's not childhood. I'm talking about a rival universe. Children live in a mythic world.

PENNY: Universe B?

PHILIP: No past. Everything free. Mythic. No wonder everything is different for these little monsters. They live in a universe that's constantly brand new. No rules. All adults try to get back to that world. But you can only do it by falling in love.

EROS: You're falling falling
          Out of Universe A
          Into Universe B
          Falling falling

(PHILIP *turns to us, three years hence*.)

PHILIP (*to us*): We had broken through. We weren't just two crazy middle-aged people. Love had got us back into a brand-new place. I swear that summer we were in the same universe with the kids.

(*Play present.*)

PENNY: I like being an adult.

PHILIP: One isn't better than the other. The kids have their universe. But we have the best of both. We can go back and forth.

EROS: Is this the moment
         You think you're gifted
         To see the present
         Annihilate the past?

PENNY: But I wouldn't mind having a little less past. Universe B.

PHILIP: We're free. Kids! Come on! Fall in!

(PHILIP *embraces* PENNY. *A deep profound kiss.*)

EROS: This is the moment
         You think you're gifted
         To see the present
         Outweigh the past
         You find your true selves
         In that precious moment
         Grace touches you
         I move in too

(*They sigh and make that palms-up gesture. Then* THE KIDS *run on with their bags.*)

PENNY: Kids! This is it! Welcome to the dig!

PHILIP: La Muculufa! This is home!

PENNY: That's our office and our stone house. Now everybody take your bags down to the stone house. That's where we all stay. Your names are on the doors! Everybody follow Icarus!

(*The* KIDS *run off with their bags.*
PHILIP *and* PENNY *turn to us, three years hence.*)

PENNY (*to us*): That summer, we were both archaeologists working on a dig at La Muculufa.

PHILIP (*to us*): I'm sure La Muculufa still rises high out of a flat plain, two limestone spires jutting into the sky.

PENNY (*to us*): Its cliffs dotted with caves

PHILIP (*to us*): The space between the two stone fingers contained our archaeological site lined with trenches. Things were very simple that summer. Everything could be solved by asking the computer three basic questions: what is it for? how old is it? what is it?

PENNY (*to us*): We fed our results into our computers

PHILIP (*to us*): Sent the data back to California

PENNY (*to us*): I loved when Philip said the next part

PHILIP (*to us*): and thanks to the network of satellites scattered above us in the sky, the world for us had become one vast archaeological dig. The Past Present annihilated. Distances all one.

PENNY (*to us*): —one vast archaeological dig. When Philip said that, my heart stood still. I looked up above me. I belonged to the world.

(PENNY *buries pieces of ancient pots and beads.*)

PENNY (*to us*): We hid pots and beads for the kids to find. Sort of a Bronze Age Easter egg hunt.

(PHILIP *maps out a site with posts and string.*)

PHILIP (*to us*): We marked off an area with string for the kids to dig.

(THE KIDS *reassemble, carrying yellow pails and shovels.*)

PENNY: Kids! Look at this bead! Pure Crete! Rare routes of the Mediterranean. How did this bead which we know is from Crete get all the way up here?

TEDDY: When's lunch?

PENNY: Apollo, darling, we will have *pranzo* as soon as we've made at least one archaeological discovery.

PHILIP: Wait till you see what work we're part of.

PENNY (*to* THE CHILDREN): What work *you're* part of.

PHILIP: Why did this bead from the island of Crete end up here in Sicily in 1100 B.C.? It's as simple as this. This is a burial site.

HALCY: You brought us to a cemetery?

PHILIP: Penny, I think they're ready to start digging. Let's start digging!

(*They begin digging.*)

PENNY: Now you must be careful. See the layers of earth? An inch of earth can represent hundreds of years' difference from the inch of earth below it.

PHILIP: It's like you're in this incredibly delicate lasagna. All layers. You are in the field!

PENNY: Be careful. It's holy—

HALCY: Is this where you were married?

SARAH: You were married *here?*

PENNY: No, Arethusa, we were married in Paris. Why not dig over here? (*She finds a pot.*) Look! I found this beautiful pot!

PHILIP: Wow!

PENNY: This is going to be a valuable day!

PHILIP: Look! Look! I found a bead!

SARAH: Beads?

LYLE: Beads?

JANE: Beads?

PENNY: We're here for the beads.

SARAH: You broke up our family for beads?

JANE: Pots? You broke up our family for pots?

TEDDY: Pots?

ROGER: Pots?

ROBIN: Beads?

LYLE: Pots and beads?

PETER: Beads and pots?

LYLE: How did you really meet Daddy?

TEDDY: Yeah, how did you meet Daddy?

SARAH: Yeah! How did you meet Daddy?

PENNY: Arethusa, I bet if you dug over here you might find—

JANE: Is it true you lied to us when you said you went to a college reunion and you really went off with Philip?

SARAH: Is it true you lied to us when you said you went to a college reunion and you really went off with Penny?

PHILIP: How are we doing down there?

TEDDY: Did you lie when you told us you met Penny in April?

PETER: Because you told us March.

PENNY: In that general period. Kids! Look! Here's another piece of pottery sticking right out! Didn't somebody find this? Daedalus? This is yours.

JANE: When did you meet? April or March?

PENNY: Everything happened so quickly. The divorce. Moving. All this. Down here, kids!

(PENNY *and* PHILIP *climb down into the trench.* THE KIDS *are above.*)

SARAH: March or April?

JANE: April or March?

ALL THE KIDS: March or April?
          April or March?
          March or April?
          April or March?

PHILIP: We met in March.

SARAH: So you lied about April.

TEDDY: Daddy lied!

SARAH: You lied?

HALCY: Did you lie, Mommy?

LYLE: You lied?

PETER: You're not supposed to lie!

ROBIN: Liar!

ROGER: Liar!

ALL THE KIDS: Liar! Liar!

PENNY: Nobody lied!

PHILIP: In another life we were lovers.

PENNY: Don't make it sound like a reincarnation experience.

PHILIP: It was another life.

PENNY: If young is considered another life—

PHILIP: Let's tell the kids this part—

PENNY: We are not liars. That's a terrible thing to say. No one is liars.

PHILIP: Let me? (*She defers.*) In another life—we were lovers. University.

PENNY: The sad part. We lost each other.

PHILIP: The happy part. We found each other. Years later.

(PHILIP *lifts* PENNY *out of the trench and then follows her.*)

PENNY: The kind of story everyone loves. Mythic—love lasting over the decades

EROS: The kind of story everyone loves
             Mythic love
             Lasting over the decades love
             Centuries love
             Oh, I forgot
             Eternal love

(THE KIDS *sit.*)

PHILIP: I was an academic.

PENNY: Me. Housewife. Exit Four. Connecticut turnpike.

PHILIP: One day I flew east and gave a lecture at the Met.

PENNY: I attended to see how fat he had become.

PHILIP: Fat!

SARAH: Daddy fat! Never!

TEDDY: Never!

LYLE: Never!

PENNY: He came out on that platform at the museum to lecture about Sicily and my heart stopped. He could've been on television.

PHILIP: Television!

PENNY: Public television. Archaeology in Action. You made Sicily come alive.

PHILIP: Q&A period after

PENNY: Doctor McKenzie, I'd like to ask you if—

PHILIP (*as* PENNY'*s mouth moves*): My God. Is that—it can't be— Penny? I heard Penny had married some real— (*He looks at* PENNY'*s* KIDS) —important distinguished congressman.

HALCY: That's Daddy!

JANE: Daddy!

PETER: Daddy!

ROBIN: *My* daddy!

ROGER: *My* daddy!

PHILIP: Had left archaeology. Had a passel of children but she's—

EROS: Bellissima issima issima issima

PHILIP: beautiful!

PENNY (*resumes*): if you were familiar with the use of computer technology to determine the trade routes of the ancient Mediterranean kingdoms?

PHILIP: Well . . . Your question bears explanation that would take up time from . . . Could we meet after the session? Next question?

(PENNY *smiles.*)

WAYNE: Where did you go?

HALCY: When did you meet again?

PENNY: Well—

PHILIP: Don't tell the kids this part.

EROS: Don't tell the kids this part

PENNY: Why not? Across the street from the Met is a wonderful hotel and we had a quiet drink and

EROS: Don't tell the kids this part

PENNY: Don't tell the kids this part.

EROS: Tell them the love
         Don't tell them the lust

(PENNY *and* PHILIP *sit side by side, each with a glass of wine.*)

PHILIP: Penny, I am an archaeologist who never got into the field. I am head of an archaeology department and I have never been in the field.

PENNY: But you could take your computer anywhere!!

PHILIP: My wife. Jeanne. My kids. No. No Sicily there. You should go. You had a wonderful knack for the field. That dig in Pennsylvania.

PENNY: We dug up a seventeenth-century sleigh!

PHILIP: Hated the seventeenth century. Too recent. No, the past Past!

PENNY: The blessed beautiful past!

(PHILIP *and* PENNY *turn and look into each other's eyes.*)

EROS: Wonderful hotels have dark corners
         Pianists play love songs from another time
         Night and Day
         Under My Skin is the place I keep you
         Only Make Believe
         Lovers sit in corners

PHILIP: You said you wanted to marry an Etruscan.

PENNY: Mel is a wonderful man. Just does not possess one drop of Etruscan blood. I love him. Our kids. The most *wonderful* kids. I'm happy. I hate my life.

PHILIP: I hate my life. I feel like some mutilated Greek statue sitting at a desk. No arms. No face. No legs. No phallus.

PENNY: Oh, but you have a phallus!

EROS: Don't tell the kids this part
         Tell the kids the facts
         Don't tell them the truth
         Tell them the love
         Don't tell them the lust
         Don't tell the kids this part

(*They sit closer.*)

PHILIP: My wife has a series of lovers. Drugs. Liquor. She's got her own permanent bed at Betty Ford.
         Betty Ford won't even take her back anymore.

(PHILIP *laughs.*
PENNY *laughs.*
Then they stop.)

PENNY: I'm a very good wife. I give the support. I shake the hands. Mel runs for Congress? Sure! I raise the money. "Hello? my husband's running for Congress and if Mel is half as good in Congress as he is at home—we need your help and help means cash." I locate money for wonderful causes. "Wait! Let's have the dance in the zoo! Right in the cages! Wait! Let's have the ball right in the hospital ward. Yes! Right in the homeless shelter . . ."
         Mel cheats. Womanizes. Why is that the most derogatory word? Womanize. He cheats.
         On me.
         I'm stranded.

PHILIP: My kids—what's going to become of them? Motorcycles. California.

PENNY: The values. The emptiness. The promise they'll all be on crack. I want my kids to have a life.

PHILIP: We all have these secret identities hiding inside us.

PENNY: We don't know who we truly are.

PHILIP: What myth we all belong to.

PENNY: Occasionally, if we're lucky or grace hits us, we're transformed and our true self shines through. Don't tell the kids this part. I snap the stem of my wineglass. The wine spills over our hands. I mop the wine from his lap with my napkin.

PHILIP: Wouldn't it be crazy if we started up again?

PENNY: You live out west!

PENNY: Don't tell the kids this part. I kissed the napkin.

PHILIP: Is there a moment when all our lives are *mythic?* Are touched by grace—by God—and we start life? Is it now? Penny, look at me.

PENNY: I don't dare.

PHILIP: We have to dare.

PENNY: I've got to get home—Exit Four—

PHILIP: We've been given a gift.

PENNY: I just came into town to have lunch. Come to the museum. Things like this don't happen. Not to me.

PHILIP: Not to me.

PENNY: I hate my life.

PHILIP: I hate my life. Let's go upstairs. Don't tell the kids this part.

PENNY: The bellhop opens the door. I look into the bedroom. Then

PHILIP: Then

PENNY: Then

EROS: Don't tell the kids this part

(PENNY *and* PHILIP *stand up.*)

WAYNE: Where did you go?

HALCY: When did you meet again?

(PENNY *pauses.*)

PENNY: Across the street from the Met is a wonderful hotel and—we had a quiet drink and Philip put a travel folder down on the table. It read:

PHILIP: Welcome to Sicily.

EROS: Sicilia Sicilia Sicilia

PHILIP: HURRAY!!!!!! It's a year later!!!

PENNY: Married!!! We made it! We got our divorces! A snap! Kids! Be happy—

(*Three years hence.*)

PHILIP (*to us*): To do what you dreamed of! All those years behind a desk!

PENNY (*to us*): We were married in Paris! We had dinner on a bateau mouche sailing around the Seine by night—a moon—

PHILIP (*to us*): We had some work to do in the archaeological department of the Louvre—

PENNY (*to us*): We discovered our favorite piece in the world.

PHILIP (*to us*): A granite sculpture this high—

PENNY (*to us*): Four Baboons Adoring the Sun

PHILIP (*to us*): —like this—palms upward—nineteenth dynasty

PENNY (*to us*): —4000 years old—

(EROS *mocks the gesture*.)

EROS: Four Baboons Adoring the Sun

PHILIP (*to us*): You should see them!

PENNY (*to us*): These four baboons

PHILIP (*to us*): staring into the sun.

PENNY (*to us*): Their eyes running out of their heads with joy

PHILIP (*to us*): Their eyes burnt out because they've seen their God.

PENNY (*to us*): But they don't care.

PHILIP (*to us*): They're so happy.

PENNY (*to us*): I was so happy!

PHILIP (*to us*): I was so happy!

EROS: Four Baboons Adoring the Sun

(PENNY *and* PHILIP *return to present*.)

LYLE: Dad, did you love our mother?

PHILIP (*to* PENNY'*s* CHILDREN): Of course. But now I love *her* mother deeper than any other human being I've ever known.

JANE: Mom, did you love Daddy?

PENNY (*to* PHILIP'*s* CHILDREN): Yes, but now I love *his* father with all my heart.

PHILIP: Now we are going to take our beads and pots and march down to the stone house and have lunch.

ALL THE KIDS: Lunch!

ROGER: Did we really find the pots?

JANE: Or did you put them here?

LYLE: *I* wanted to find them.

PENNY: You *did* find them. Okay, let's go!

PHILIP: Let's go!

(*Three years hence.*)

PHILIP (*to us*): We all marched down the path to the stone house.

(*The wind plays its dangerous tremolo.*)

PENNY (*to us*): And then I heard the sound again. The wind sent voices to us like a quiet silver gift.

(*They hear voices.*)

PHILIP (*to us*): Where were the voices coming from? Not the cliffs. Not echoing out of the caves. Where? And then we turned.

PENNY (*to us*): The voices were coming from our stone house. Out of our bedroom window.

WAYNE'S VOICE: "Penny, all it is, is a challenge—"

HALCY'S VOICE: "Oh Philip Philip Philip! Are we up to it?"

WAYNE'S VOICE: I *heard* him say that too!

HALCY'S VOICE: I heard her say, "Can she hear you?"

WAYNE'S VOICE: I heard him say, "Jeanne is in the other room. Drinking."

HALCY'S VOICE: I heard her say, "Mel's at the United Nations so he claims."

WAYNE'S VOICE: I love you I love you I love you I love you I love you

HALCY'S VOICE: I love you I love you I love you I love you I
    love you

(*The sound reverberates.*
A bed appears.
Two figures under the covers.
EROS *leans over the headboard and uncovers* WAYNE *and* HALCY.)

EROS: What kept you so long?
          It's time
          I get impatient
          It's time
          I wait for everyone
          I waited for you
          Now just get to it
          It's time and now's the time

(PENNY *and* PHILIP *gingerly approach the bed.*)

PHILIP: Hi, guys.

PENNY: Anybody home?

(PENNY *and* PHILIP *pull back the covers revealing* WAYNE *and* HALCY.)

PHILIP: I think it's lovely you're getting along

PENNY: but we all have our own beds.

(WAYNE *and* HALCY *look at their parents with admiration.*)

HALCY: Mommy, you're so very *brave*.

PENNY: Let's go!

WAYNE: You believed!

HALCY: You threw away your lives!

WAYNE: You gave up everything!

HALCY: Us! You didn't care what we felt. You loved!

WAYNE: Love is the only reality. Love is all.

HALCY: Stronger than anything. Love makes us immortal!

WAYNE: You said that.

HALCY: The night of the twenty-third of March.

WAYNE: And repeated it—eleven P.M. in the evening Eastern Standard. Eight P.M. California.

HALCY: Mom! I was listening on the line when you and Philip would talk—

PENNY: You did what?

HALCY: Mom! That's how we met! I realized someone else was on the line.

(HALCY *puts her arm around* WAYNE.)

WAYNE: And that was me.

(WAYNE *leans against* HALCY.)

HALCY: We were each on the line when you and Philip would talk—

PHILIP: You knew?

WAYNE: I told the kids about every phone call and every letter.

PENNY: You told the kids?

HALCY: Everybody knew.

WAYNE: You have us to thank for helping you get together.

HALCY: We could've got in the way!

WAYNE: Refused to come.

HALCY: Refused in general!

WAYNE: But your love kept us healthy.

HALCY: I'm off drugs!

WAYNE: I'm sober! Sane!

HALCY: Your love was our love!

WAYNE: Is our love!

HALCY: We never met until the plane.

WAYNE: But we knew each other

HALCY: through you.

(*The rest of* THE KIDS *circle their parents.*)

SARAH: We knew everything and we were mad.

JANE: We knew everything!

PETER: We were mad.

LYLE: We knew it all!

TEDDY: I was really mad.

ROGER: Yeah!

ROBIN: I was very mad.

KIDS (*except* WAYNE *and* HALCY): Yea!

(WAYNE *stands up on the bed.*)

WAYNE: Stop that!
    Kids! Listen to me! I want you shaping up. I want you
    behaving well and supporting these two magnificent people.
    They are working so hard to give us a life. Now let's get it
    together! That means unpacking your bags, shaping up, and
    getting ready for lunch!

HALCY: Kids! Listen to Wayne! Oh, Mom! he's *so* wonderful!

(*The wind, the sea roars triumphantly.*
THE KIDS *march off.*
PENNY *and* PHILIP *are stunned.*)

PENNY: They were in our bed.

PHILIP: Okay. Okay. Okay. We're going to have to be strong.

PENNY: I am *strong*. They're only thirteen.

PHILIP: Don't make any big thing of it.

PENNY: Not make any big thing of it! They were under our covers in our bed! Thirteen? Is that old enough? They were taking notes! They were listening on the phone? Omigod! The monstrous things I said about their father—the things you said to me!

PHILIP: We have to figure this out—

PENNY: What I said to you! Oh God. I described *your* body to you. I described *my* body to you. I described what I felt about you. I described what it was like to be with you!

PHILIP: I just remembered. I told you I wanted you to be my wife, my nanny, my whore.

PENNY: My man. My soul. My flame. My father. My teacher. My student. My—oh my God—

PHILIP: my partner, my mistress, my inspiration—

PENNY: I can never sleep in that bed again!

(PENNY *tears the bed apart, looking.*)

PENNY: Dope? Are they smoking dope? Liquor? Are there any liquor bottles?

PHILIP: Penny. No. Wait!

PENNY: What?

PHILIP: Ask the right questions. What is it for? How old is it? What is it? Of course. The archaeological questions! We're reading it wrong—the entire situation.

PENNY: These two are being kept miles apart. Quarantine!

PHILIP: They're not sneaks! They're good kids. Keeping them apart? That's exactly what we must not do! Don't be angry at them.

PENNY: I'm not angry. I want to die. They heard everything? They can probably tell you the dates.

PHILIP: Look at the good side.

PENNY: What good side? Are we being watched right now? What are you smiling about?

PHILIP: Don't you see? What is it for? They were pretending to be us.

PENNY: Pretending to be us? This is not Pirandello.

PHILIP: Playacting. That's all.

PENNY: That's all?!

PHILIP: Don't blow this up out of perspective. What is it? They're in love with us!

PENNY: That is not healthy.

PHILIP: They want to be us! Can you imagine any greater compliment?

PENNY: Yes. Not being nasty little spies.

PHILIP: Thank God they know. Everything out in the open. Don't you feel clear and clean and good and—

PENNY: I can never look at any of my children again.

PHILIP: Penny, stop it! Let them know what adults can be about. They don't know anything about love. They've never seen love. All they knew about adults with me and Jeanne was hate and fury and rage and homicide. And what do they know about love from you and Mel? To hear anything about love can't be bad. We're the great model. We're the ideal. That's what they want to be part of. Let them know about love. They're trying to free themselves of all the unhappiness of you and Mel—me and Jeanne—

PENNY: All my kids know about adults is me and Mel being brutal to each other. The hatred they've seen till now—oh God, you're right. I'm making big stuff out of this—

PHILIP: Our kids love us! How do we sustain that? That's our main problem.

PENNY: They love us! Our children love us—my God!

PHILIP: If all our problems are this hard—

PENNY: I don't want them in each other's bed.

PHILIP: That's the easy part. How old is it? They just got off a plane. Everything brand new. These are kids who've never even been to Europe.

PENNY: Mine have. Well, London. But I guess that doesn't count.

PHILIP: The newness will wear off. Each other's beds? That's just vigilance on our part

PENNY: —and drawing lines. Yes.

PHILIP: We've got to handle this carefully. Rules.

PENNY: The way they said Beads. Pots. I want them to be thrilled by Sicily. I want them to see Sicily through our eyes. To see its grandeur. Its majesty—I don't want them *laughing* at us.

PHILIP: Let's let them see temples. The tourist Sicily. Let them see the flashy stuff so they can focus in on what *we're* doing. Kids! They're in love with us! Now let's have them fall in love with Sicily. Kids! We're going on a camping trip. Now.

PENNY: Now?

PHILIP: Right now.

PENNY: They just got off a plane!

PHILIP: I don't care! I don't care! Kids! We're going on a trip!

(THE KIDS *cheer.*
They all crowd into the van.
They drive.)

EROS: Attenzione Prego
                    Taoramina

PENNY: Taoramina.

(THE CHILDREN *echo the names of the cities.*)

EROS: Siracusa

PHILIP: Siracusa

EROS: Agrigento

PENNY: Agrigento

EROS: Segesta

PHILIP: Segesta

EROS: Selinunte

PENNY: Selinunte

(THE KIDS *are exhausted.*)

EROS: Monreale

PHILIP: Monreale

EROS: Bagheria

PENNY: Bagheria

EROS: Cefalù

PHILIP: Cefalù

EROS: Erice!

PENNY AND PHILIP: Erice!

PENNY (*to us*): And it was evening. Above us, built on sheer cliffs, the town of Erice.

PHILIP: Dedicated to what goddess?

PENNY: Astarte.

PHILIP: And who is Astarte?

EROS: Astarte is Aphrodite
               Aphrodite is Venus

PENNY: Astarte is Aphrodite.

JANE: I'm Aphrodite.

PHILIP: Kid, this is your town.

(PHILIP *lights a fire.*
Time change.)

JANE: But what did you wear?

PENNY: I sent you photos of the wedding.

PETER: Mommy had a white dress with a veil and white shoes and blue ribbons in her hair.

SARAH: You wore white! That's a laugh.

PENNY: That's right, Sarah, it is a laugh! Anything you want to know about the wedding—ask Peter—

(*Time change.*)

          Okay, kids—postcard time!

JANE: Dear Daddy I love Sicily

LYLE: Dear Mommy we saw temples

SARAH: Dear Everyone wish you were here

PETER: Dear Daddy we had pizza

TEDDY: Dear Mommy I love Penny

ROBIN: Dear Daddy I love Philip

PHILIP: What amazing kids!

JANE: I love archaeology.

PHILIP: What do you like the best?

JANE: That nobody knows anything about the past. That you make it all up.

LYLE: Yeah. You make it all up!

SARAH: An archaeologist is like being a detective.

ROGER: It's like being in a mystery story.

PHILIP: That's right. Finding the clues to make sense out of history—

(*Time change.*)

SARAH (*screams*): Look!

(THE KIDS *sit up and point out into the audience.*)

LYLE: Look!

ROGER: Who are they?

PETER: Is that the Mafia?

JANE: Daddy said the Mafia lived here.

PHILIP: Just sit quiet. Don't look at them.

PENNY: Don't tell them that—

ROBIN: I don't like the Mafia.

TEDDY: I know about the Mafia.

LYLE: Are they going to kill us?

SARAH: I'm calling Mommy immediately!

JANE: I want Daddy.

PHILIP'S KIDS: Mommy! Mommy! Mommy!

PENNY'S KIDS: Daddy! Daddy! Daddy!

PHILIP: A very wise person told me there's only one thing to know about Sicily. Don't make eye contact with anything— Because if you do, it'll bite you!

PENNY: No! Look life in the eye! Eye contact in spades! Don't frighten the kids. You can see what it is. It's hardly Lucky Luciano.

PHILIP (*looking out*): Oh. It's just a band of ragged Sicilian children.

PENNY: Not lucky like you.

PHILIP: These little ragazzi have no homes—

PENNY: Don't be afraid. Join us. Avanti! (*Waves into darkness.*) Ciao, bambini!

PHILIP: Benvenuto!

PENNY: Buona sera!

PHILIP: Salve! Mangiare?

PENNY: We have food left. Cioccolata? Don't run away!

(*Silence.*
The ocean.)

TEDDY: Was that the Mafia?

ROGER: Mafia?!!

ALL THE KIDS: Mafia?!!

PENNY: No, it wasn't. Everybody calm. Besides, the Mafia here is good. The one in America is bad.

SARAH: Why did the Mafia become bad?

PHILIP: Why do you think?

SARAH: I don't know

LYLE: I don't know

PETER: I don't know

TEDDY: I don't know

JANE: I don't know

ROBIN: I don't know

ROGER: I don't know

PHILIP: But, my darlings, in Sicily that is the only answer. I *do* not know. Learn that and you have learned the most—the *only*—rule in Sicily. *Omertà*. It means Silence. Say after me. O. Mer. Ta.

KIDS: O. Mer.

PHILIP (*in a mock rage*): Shh. *Silence!* You never *say* Omertà. Omertà *is* Silence. One never tells. With the mouth. With the eyes.

PENNY: With the postcards. With the phone calls home.

PHILIP: And you know what the greatest sin is? Infamita! The Breaking of the Family Silence. Are we a family?

KIDS: Yes.

PENNY: Yes! We're a family.

PHILIP: And you know what happens to you when you break the family silence and commit *Infamita?*

(PHILIP *slices his throat.*
THE KIDS *scream.*)

PHILIP: Remember Omertà. The most important word. Every family has its secrets. What happens here stays here. Omertà.

PENNY: Or else your civilization will crumble.

PHILIP: The Breaking of the Silence. Say after me. In. Fa. Mi. Ta.

(THE KIDS *start to speak, then realize they should keep mum.*)

PHILIP: Smart kids. Welcome to Sicily.

PENNY: Kids! We want to give you a life—not of privilege

PHILIP: —but of possibilities

PENNY: —not a life where you can *buy* what's of value.

PHILIP: We want to put all these treasures in you.

HALCY: Treasures? I have treasures in me?

PENNY: That's why we're here. To release those treasures. In you. In you. In you. And you and you and you. In all of you. In Philip. In me. You can laugh at those silly myths in that stupid book. People transformed into trees. Into birds. But we have become transformed. We have become a family and families become civilizations. You are not the same kids who got on that plane in America last night. You are transformed. You may not feel it. But it's beginning. I'm so glad you're all here. Now everybody up. Get in your sleeping bags.

(PHILIP *puts out the fire.*
Each of THE KIDS *except* WAYNE *climbs into a sleeping bag in a circle around* PENNY *and* PHILIP's *double sleeping bag set in the center.*)

PHILIP: Tomorrow we're up at dawn to be on our way. But right now I want to teach you all an old Sicilian folk song. We are going to sing together.

(PHILIP *sings a trick version of "Take Me Out to the Ball Game" starting it one beat earlier so it ends one beat short, which makes* THE KIDS *laugh contentedly.*
PHILIP *sees* WAYNE *standing at the edge of the circle looking out to the sea and walks down to his son.*)

EROS: Icarus stands on a beach
        Daedalus warns Icarus of the sun
        The sun
        Don't listen to Daedalus
        Fly higher
        Higher
        Into the sun

PHILIP: Into bed—

WAYNE: I took a walk by myself before to figure some things out and I was hungry and I looked down and there was a bush with big juicy berries on it and I ate all the berries. The world took care of me. I'm so happy here.

PHILIP: You must show me the bush with all the berries on it.

WAYNE: I'm sorry I crawled in your suitcase when you were leaving. I didn't want anything to change. But now I see that's the best part of life. Of my life. Everything changes all the time.

PHILIP: I'm so happy you're here. Into bed.

(PHILIP *hugs his son.*
WAYNE *climbs into his bag.*
PENNY *and* PHILIP *climb into their double sleeping bag.*)

PENNY: Good night . . .

(*Silence.*)

LYLE (*calls out*): Daddy, how did you and Penny meet?

PHILIP: What are you going to be when you grow up? A little tax accountant?

PENNY: At a museum. Back to bed.

PETER (*calls out*): Mommy wore a white dress with a veil and white shoes and blue ribbons in her hair.

PENNY: That's right, Peter. Very good. Nighty night. Say Ciao.

WAYNE: Ciao

HALCY: Ciao

LYLE: Ciao

(PENNY *counts off each kid on her fingers.*)

SARAH: Ciao

JANE: Ciao

PETER: Ciao

TEDDY: Ciao

ROBIN: Ciao

(*Pause*)

ROGER: Ciao

(*Pause*)

JANE: Mommy? I love archaeology.

(*Silence.
Peace.*)

PENNY: A child. Should we have a child?

PHILIP: Another child?

PENNY: I'm serious. A child from us?

(PENNY *and* PHILIP *embrace.*)

EROS: One more child
           To mark our love
           Yes a child
           This idea fills your head
           Possesses your body
           I do not control

> I offer a choice
> I say to your soul
> Rejoice Rejoice re—

(PENNY *sits up, very happy, very satisfied.*)

PENNY: Everything is going to be okay.

EROS: Beware the gods
          We're all around you

PENNY (*listens to* THE KIDS): I think they're quiet. Yes. Perfect
. . . Philip?

PHILIP: Yes?

PENNY: La Muculufa. I wish our dig didn't sound like a South
American dance craze.

PHILIP: What are you talking about?

PENNY: Now hold on. What if we've been reading the site
wrong—

PHILIP: Wrong?

PENNY: Maybe those limestone caves and cliffs are not some vast
mortuary with these elaborate mysterious burial ceremo-
nies—

PHILIP: It's a burial site. Everybody says La Muculufa is a burial
site and it doesn't sound like a dance craze—

PENNY: Maybe it *isn't* a burial site. Maybe it's a place where
women came to give *birth*. To offer their children at birth
to the goddess of fertility.

PHILIP: All the evidence is of death—the underworld—

PENNY: Childbirth takes you near death—

PHILIP: The chance is—one in a million. Less than that.

PENNY: All I'm saying is let's look at La Muculufa in a new way.

(*Suddenly,* THE KIDS *sit up, terrified.*)

PHILIP (*to us*): And then we heard the rumbling.

(EROS *appears gleefully.*)

EROS: Rocks split
             Earth shakes
             Ground moves
             Air burns

PENNY: Everybody! Hang on!

ROBIN: Disneyland!

(*The earth splits.*
Smoke pours out of the sudden gash in the earth.
PENNY *and* PHILIP *herd their* KIDS *under their sleeping bag.*
In the panic, WAYNE *and* HALCY *run off unseen by the others.*
Sudden silence.
PHILIP *lowers the sleeping bag.*)

JANE: Smell the air

SARAH: It's burning

PENNY: The air was on fire.

PHILIP: Look! Goats! Sheep! Running along the beach!

ROGER: Was that an earthquake?

PENNY: The cliffs could've caved in!

TEDDY: Are we killed?

LYLE: California! The big bang!

PHILIP: We are so lucky! We could've been buried! We've got
    to get back to the dig. Let's go—hurry up!

(PENNY *and* PHILIP *collect everyone's sleeping bags and begin hurling*
them off.
THE KIDS *peer into the gaping crevasse in the earth.*)

PENNY: We're all fine. Models of coraggio. We're all here. You all behaved very well. Grace under pressure! Are all the children here? Where's Halcy? Wayne?

PHILIP: We've got to get back to the dig.

PENNY: Let's make sure everything is all right here first. Wayne? Halcy?

PHILIP: I want to make sure everything is all right at the dig.

PENNY: Oh, this comes second? Wayne? Halcy?

(HALCY and WAYNE appear out of the night.)

HALCY: Mother. We want to speak to you.

WAYNE: We have something to ask you.

HALCY: We want your permission to spend the night together.

WAYNE: Your blessing.

PENNY: Philip. Would you please handle this?

PHILIP: This can wait.

WAYNE: This cannot wait! There's an earthquake. Suppose we all died?

HALCY: So little time. That's what you said to Philip. I saw the letter! April sixteenth.

PENNY: What I said to Philip on April sixteenth was my own business.

WAYNE: I've never spent the night with anybody. She wants to spend it with me.

PHILIP: No!

PENNY: You're kids!

WAYNE: Will you let us live together?

PENNY: No! Yes, we are all living together.

HALCY: Mom? Don't you want me to be as happy as you?

WAYNE: I drank because I wanted to be happy.

HALCY: I took drugs because I wanted to be happy.

WAYNE: But I never saw anybody happy till you.

PENNY: You have the rest of your life to be happy.

HALCY: You hurt Daddy.

PENNY: Your daddy hurt me. He was unfaithful. He put his career over everything.

WAYNE (*to* PHILIP): That's what Mom said about *you*.

PENNY: If I stayed with your father one more day I would have got cancer and suffocated and died.

HALCY: That will happen to me if I don't sleep with Wayne.

PENNY: That will *not* happen to you if you don't sleep with Wayne.

WAYNE: Dad, I want what you have! What's wrong with that?

PHILIP: You are not going to do this.

HALCY: Am I so awful and worthless and ugly and stupid I can't touch your precious Philip's son?

WAYNE: Aren't I good enough for her, Dad? Am I such an asshole?

PHILIP: You are children.

WAYNE: I am not a child!

PHILIP: Oh, yes you are! You are thirteen years old! We are going back to La Muculufa to see if the quake hit the dig. The computers are incredibly delicate—

PENNY: It's all jet lag and brand new and I appreciate and am touched that you understand what Philip and I are trying to build, but get your asses into that van!

WAYNE: Will you let us live together as you?

PHILIP: No!

PENNY: Yes! You are living together—

WAYNE: Yes? No? No? Yes? Are you lying to us?

HALCY: Do you wish you had always been together?

PHILIP: Yes!

PENNY: No!

HALCY: Why?

PENNY: Because then I wouldn't have you!

WAYNE: Did you hate everyone before you found each other?

PENNY: Yes.

PHILIP: No.

WAYNE: Did you hate Mom?

HALCY: Did you hate Dad?

PENNY: No.

PHILIP: Yes.

WAYNE: Back in California you always came home late.

PHILIP: I was busy supporting you!

WAYNE: Tell us the truth. Did you ever hate your life so much you wanted to die?

PENNY: Yes!

PHILIP: No!

HALCY: Did you have affairs before each other?

PENNY: No!

PHILIP: Yes!

HALCY: Who?

JANE: Who?

PHILIP: Wanda Hess.

SARAH: Mrs. Hess! Yuk!

PHILIP: You want truth? Let's get it all out.

PENNY: You never told me about any Wanda Hess.

TEDDY: Steven Hess's mother?

SARAH: You made me related to Steven Hess?

PHILIP: Screwing Wanda Hess does not involve you.

PENNY: Who is Wanda Hess?

WAYNE: When did you and Mrs. Hess happen?

PHILIP: Four years ago for two horrible years.

PENNY: You never told me about Wanda Hess.

PHILIP: Some woman in my department.

PENNY: An archaeologist?

PHILIP: From an entirely different period. The Sumerians.

PENNY: I don't know anything about the Sumerians.

PHILIP: Neither did Wanda Hess. Okay—everybody in the van!

HALCY: I thought you were different. You haven't changed. You're the same in Sicily as you were on Exit Four. I'll call Father and ask him if we can spend the night together. He'll understand!

PENNY: You are not to tell your father anything that is going on here. You understand? This is omertà in spades.

(PENNY *draws her hand across her throat.*
EROS *steps between* WAYNE *and* HALCY.
Everyone freezes in place.)

EROS: One new child
             To mark your love
             Yes a child
             This idea fills your head
             Possesses your body
             One new child

(*Time resumes.*)

HALCY: We almost died! Just now!

PENNY: You know what I think? It's disgusting. You're too young. You're brother and sister. Fratella e fratello.

HALCY: We are not fratello fratella. We just met on a plane!

WAYNE: Yes! We want to give you a child.

PHILIP: Wayne!

HALCY: We want to give the new family its own child. You're too old to have children.

SARAH: You're too old!

LYLE: You're too old!

JANE: You're too old!

PETER: Too old!

ROGER: Too old!

ROBIN: Too old!

ALL THE KIDS: Too old!

PHILIP: Halcy, you leave my son alone! Do you have drugs? What are you selling to my boy?!

PENNY: My daughter is hardly a drug pusher! Your alcoholic son can't keep it in his pants long enough to get through puberty!

HALCY: Did you tell Philip that I smoked pot?

WAYNE: Did you tell Penny that I drank liquor?

PHILIP: Just look at her. She's a brutal, crass, drug-crazed creature who takes what she wants—

PENNY: Johnnie Walker Black Label learned it somewhere—

PHILIP: Wayne is nothing like me! Take that back!

(PHILIP *raises his hand to* PENNY.
Then pulls back.
But it's too late.)

PENNY: Is that what you did to *her?*

SARAH: Penny, he hit Mommy!

LYLE: Mommy hit him!

PHILIP: Penny. I'm so sorry.

PENNY: Don't you come near me. I see why Jeanne had to take drugs. And drink. Jeanne was terrified of you!

PHILIP: Penny, look at me. I'm so sorry.

LYLE: Dad, you sound just like mother

SARAH: when you told her you were leaving.

JANE: Mom, you sound just like Daddy

ROGER, PETER, ROBIN: when you told him you were leaving.

PENNY: I do not sound anything like your father!

PHILIP: I don't sound anything like your mother!

JANE: Are you two getting divorced?

PETER: Who takes care of us?

JANE: Where do we go?

PETER: Daddy's away with his secretary.

LYLE: Mommy's in the rehab

ROBIN: Grandpa's dead!

ROGER: Grandma's dead!

SARAH: Where do we go?

TEDDY: Who feeds us?

LYLE: Who buys me clothes?

PHILIP: Shut up! I should set you loose like those Sicilian raga-muffins! Learn independence! Can't you do anything on your own? You're not cripples!

PENNY: And Wayne and Halcy want to be us?

PHILIP: Good Christ, they're us and we've become Mel and Jeanne. It's just like home.

PENNY: Shut up. It *is* home.

LYLE: Home . . .

TEDDY: Do you want to know all the card games I can't play? I can't play bridge. I can't play poker. I can't play gin. I can't play canasta. And Mommy says it's your fault.

(*Time freezes again.*
EROS *studies* WAYNE *and* HALCY.)

EROS: Come taste the gift
          The gods gave to man
          Up there in that cliff
          Is the cave where it all began

Come be the first
Ever to know the joy
The moon shows you the way
Happy girl
Happy boy

(EROS *signals* WAYNE *and* HALCY.
WAYNE *and* HALCY *stand hand in hand and then are gone.*)

PHILIP: Now we're going to pack up and

PENNY: Let's get to it! Andiamo!

(*Three years hence.*)

PENNY (*to us*): And in that moment, was it my eyes? Was it the
night—Wayne and Halcy vanished.

PHILIP (*to us*): They stepped into the dark.

(*Play returns to present.*)

PENNY: Halcy? Wayne? Where are you? Come back! Where are
they!

SARAH: They're up there! Going up the cliff!

KIDS: Up there! Up there!

EROS: The children scale the cliffs
               The children find a path
               The children dig their hands into the earth
               They climb higher
               Higher

(WAYNE *and* HALCY *appear, climbing a cliff.*
Everyone scatters.)

PENNY: Kids! Wait! Let's stay together.

LYLE'S VOICE: Wayne??

JANE'S VOICE: Halcy???

ROGER'S VOICE: Mommy!

TEDDY'S VOICE: Daddy!

EROS: The children scale the cliffs
The children find a path
The children dig their hands into the earth
Icarus climbs higher
Higher
Higher
Higher

(*Silence.*)

PENNY: Moonlight. The cliffs! Which way to go?

PHILIP: I find a path, thick with red flowers.

PENNY: I see Wayne and Halcy in the distance. Hello!

PHILIP: Wait. We see them pulling off their clothes, leaving a trail behind them.

PENNY: I scramble after them like a guerrilla on their trail.

PHILIP: The night air is thick with the buzzing of bees

PENNY: in panic from the earthquake. Heat. The air on fire.

PETER'S VOICE: Where are you?

ROBIN'S VOICE: I'm frightened!

SARAH'S VOICE: Daddy?

PENNY: Look! Wayne and Halcy ahead of us are naked

PHILIP: Get back here!

PENNY: in and out of our sight. Up the cliff! Where are they?

PHILIP: They vanish behind a stone column.

EROS: Of course it's by moonlight.

(*Three years hence.*)

PENNY (*to us*): I came around the column first. The moon was
    quite bright. I expected to see our kids doing something
    horrible and I'd spank them and lecture them and separate
    them and send one of them back to America. But I heard
    that sound again—and this is what I saw. I swear to you on
    my soul after all these years that this is what I saw that night
    behind that column. My Halcy. Little Wayne. I saw our
    children—yes—making love and then in front of my eyes I
    saw them transformed.

(*Play returns to present.*)

EROS: Wayne

PENNY: Wayne? Halcy?

EROS: Halcy
    The moon reflects in the pool of water
    The pool says Yes
    I am Halcy

(*Vision: The only naturalistic detail. Superreal. Like a Magritte. A deer
drinks out of a pool of water.*)

    The deer says Yes
    I am Wayne
    The spring bubbles yes yes yes

(*The deer looks up.
Then the vision is gone.
Three years hence.*)

PHILIP (*to us*): I came around the column.
    Over there, I saw a deer. Yes, I saw a spring.
    But over *there*, I saw two inept kids going at it in some
    insane parody of Penny and me. Universe A? Universe B?
    Instead of our getting into the kids' world, we had dragged
    the kids into our world. For all our ideals, we had passed
    only our fever on to our children. I want life to have passion
    but I also want life to be sane. I started to run forward to stop
    them but Penny pulled me back.

(*Play returns to present.*)

PENNY: They are magnificent!

PHILIP: Are you crazy?

PENNY: What happened to them is what happened to us—
They were there—where are they?

PETER'S VOICE: Where are you?

ROBIN'S VOICE: I'm frightened!

SARAH'S VOICE: Daddy?

LYLE, SARAH, TEDDY: Daddy? Daddy?

PHILIP: Kids! Here we are! Penny, we have other kids to care
for—

(*Music: Ominous, driven.*)

PENNY: Wayne! Halcy! They're gone—where are they?

PHILIP: We find our way out of the forest. Kids!
Kids! We come to the road that goes up the cliff.
There is a procession.

(*In the distance a procession.*
Torches.
Incense.)

PENNY: What feast day is this?

PHILIP: What feast day is this in the middle of the night to make
the crowd sing so mournfully?

PENNY: The town celebrates escape from an earthquake.

PHILIP: An old man carries an enormous cross carved out of
gnarled twisted wood.

PENNY: Altar boys aroused from sleep swing gold thuribles of
burning incense.

PHILIP: Pregnant women march to the top of cliffs where the temple of Astarte once stood holding rosaries over their bellies.

PENNY: They pray for their children.

PHILIP: They pray for unborn children.

KIDS: Look! Look! Look!

(WAYNE *and* HALCY *appear at a height*.)

EROS: Icarus stands on the cliff
             Icarus looks down at the sea
             The sea
             Icarus is ready to fly

PHILIP: Wayne! You get down here!

PENNY: Halcy! Not so close.

PHILIP: Hey, kids. Now get away from the edge.

PENNY: What are they saying? I can't hear.

PHILIP: You get down here—you will never see each other again.

PENNY: No no—I won't let that happen! You should be together! Come down! I'm on your side!

WAYNE: Dad, we are so happy!

PHILIP: Wayne? What are you saying?

WAYNE: Halcy, give me your hand.

(*Three years hence*.)

PHILIP (*to us*): Wayne reached out to take Halcy's hand.

PENNY (*to us*): But Halcy pulled her hand away and stepped back from the edge of the cliff.

PHILIP (*to us*): Wayne looked at her, looked down at us, looked at the sky.

PENNY (*to us*): Wayne stepped forward into space.

(*Play returns to present.*)

PHILIP: Wayne!

PENNY: Halcy!

(*They rush forward.*
WAYNE *falls slowly through the sky.*)

EROS: Wayne who was Icarus dreaming of flight
      Steps into the sky
      But it is moonlight and he wears no wings
      No sunlight melts the wings
      Wayne falls through the sky
      The saddest song I ever did hear
      Dido's lament
      This is sadder
      Wayne falls through the sky

(HALCY *reaches out.*)

HALCY: Wayne!

ROGER: Wayne leaps over the side

ROBIN: Wayne can do anything

JANE: Wayne is my hero

PETER: See Wayne fly

LYLE: I love you, Wayne

TEDDY: Let's follow Wayne.

HALCY: Wayne!

SARAH: See Wayne against the moon . . .

EROS: "When I am laid
      Am laid in earth,
      May my wrongs create no trouble
      No trouble in my breast"

The saddest song I ever did hear
Dido's lament
This is sadder
Wayne steps over the edge
Wayne falls through the sky

(PHILIP *falls to his knees.*
PENNY *comforts him.*
EROS *appears carrying* WAYNE'*s body.*)

EROS: "When I am laid, am laid in earth,
May my wrongs create no trouble
No trouble in my breast.
Remember me, remember me
But ah! forget my fate"

(EROS *descends triumphantly into the earth,* WAYNE'*s body in his arms.*
PHILIP *screams in agony.*
The scream reverberates through the night,
THE CHILDREN *come forward and kneel.*
PENNY *embraces* PHILIP.
Then cold light.
Three years hence.)

PENNY (*to us*): We got back to the dig. There was a fax. My kids' father was getting married. Mel wanted his children at the wedding.

(*Play returns to present. The children stand.*)

JANE: We talked to Dad

PETER: Daddy wants us home

ROBIN: Daddy's getting married

JANE: Daddy wants us to be part of his new life

ROGER: Daddy's getting married

PETER: Daddy's in love

JANE: I want to go to Wayne's funeral

PENNY: You can't go to Wayne's funeral. Daddy's getting married the same day back east. Daddy won't—Daddy *can't* change the wedding day. Daddy wants you there.

ROGER: Can you come to Daddy's wedding?

ROBIN: Yes! Come to Daddy's wedding!

PENNY: No. Go upstairs and pack your suitcases.

LYLE: We came here on Friday

JANE: Today is Sunday

ROGER: I thought we'd stay longer

(ROGER *goes*.)

SARAH: You came here for beads?

(SARAH *goes*.)

LYLE: You threw away our lives for beads?

JANE: Wayne died for beads?

(LYLE *and* SARAH *and* ROBIN *and* PETER *and* TEDDY *leave*. HALCY *remains*.
Three years hence.)

PENNY (*to us*): The kids asked the questions I've asked myself over and over since that summer. The questions the police asked. An autopsy showed no drugs. No alcohol. He was clean. He was sane. He was healthy. He was happy! Wayne meant to die? Wayne wanted to die with Halcy? The police finally wrote down "Incidente." Just an accident.

(*Play returns to present*.

PENNY *comforts* HALCY. PHILIP, *in a quiet rage, watches them*.)

PHILIP: Why do you have a child and I don't?

PENNY: Couldn't you say you're happy Halcy is alive?

PHILIP: I'm not.

PENNY: Halcy, go up and pack your bags. You have to go to your father's wedding.

HALCY: Is Wayne's body going to be on the plane with us? I want to ride with Wayne.

PHILIP: My wife—Jeanne—Wayne's mother does not want to see you. Because this is what she will ask you. Why didn't you jump?

HALCY: Yes. Why am I alive? I should've jumped. I loved him.

PENNY: What are you saying! Both of you!

PHILIP: Are you a coward? You should've jumped!

PENNY: She did not jump because she is not crazy!

PHILIP: Oh. My boy is crazy?

PENNY: She had a moment of sanity. Halcy, go up and pack.

HALCY: I made love to Wayne.
    Do you think I'll have a baby?
    If I don't no one will ever know Wayne.
    You're too old to have children.
    I had my one chance.

PENNY: Darling, you'll have other chances. Whatever happens, we'll see this through. Whatever happens, no one is going to forget Wayne. No one can take Wayne away from you.

(HALCY *starts to go*.)

PHILIP: Wait. What did Wayne say to you up there on the cliff?

HALCY: Up there, we were perfect.
    Wayne said life would never be better than it was that moment.
    Wayne took my hand. But I pulled back.

PENNY: Thank God you did pull back.

HALCY: I loved him. I'll never get over this. I'll live to be a hundred years old and never get over that I didn't take his hand. I had one chance to be a goddess. Now all I'll be the rest of my life is this. Like everyone else. I hate this. Mom. I hate this. Me. I hate my life. I hate life.

PENNY: You don't. Don't say that. You don't.

(HALCY *goes*.)

PHILIP: All your kids look like their father. It's like having ghosts of your former life all around us. A child? A child from us? Wayne's death—that's our only child.

PENNY: She's your stepdaughter. Wayne is my stepson. We're all together. Can't tell who's yours and can't tell who's mine. You said that. Grief is like love. It makes us say terrible things.

PHILIP: I hate emotions. Hate them. Hate them.

PENNY: Philip—

PHILIP: Who is Mel marrying?

PENNY: Not one of the bimbos.
He's marrying his secretary.
She's plausible.
She makes wonderful reservations.
She got us here.

PHILIP: What kind of name is Halcy?

PENNY: For halcyon.

PHILIP: You named your kid after a drug?

PENNY: Not the drug. The happiness. Halcyon days.

PHILIP: You and Mel had halcyon days?

PENNY: Mel and I had halcyon days!

PHILIP: And she was born. Halcyon days.

PENNY: Wayne?

PHILIP: For John Wayne.

PENNY: John Wayne!

PHILIP: Months before he was born he kicked like a cowboy and we got to calling the unborn baby John Wayne—and when he was born, we realized he already had been named. We had no choice. Even if he was a girl. John Wayne.

PENNY: John Wayne. Not the best name for a girl.

(*He looks at her then comes to her and kisses her ferociously.*
She responds.
He pulls back.)

PHILIP: I was so happy back at the university dreaming about being here. Dreaming about you. You know what I miss? I miss dreaming of all this. It's sort of right, flying back with the kids, back to my wife hating every minute of it. And I'll spend the entire trip dreaming of you. Dreaming of here. Wishing I could have life.

PENNY: But we have it!

PHILIP: But it's not real. I'm not coming back.

PENNY: I've given up everything to come here.

PHILIP: You belong here. I don't. You actually like making eye contact. No matter what the risks are. I don't. You'd make a leap into space! Wayne's like you. Halcy's like me.

PENNY: Like everyone else.

PHILIP: And there's nothing wrong with that.

(*In the distance car horn beeps.*
THE KIDS *yell,* "Mommy!" "Daddy!")

PHILIP: The children are coming with me?

FOUR BABOONS ADORING THE SUN

PENNY: My children are not coming with you . . .

PHILIP: They have to.
Their father is getting married.
They have to go to the wedding.

PENNY: My children can choose.
Who's staying with me.
Who's going to their father's wedding.

(*Pause*)

PHILIP: Come back with me to the university?

(*Pause*)

PENNY: Never. I am here.

(*Pause*)

PHILIP: Does Mel's new wife have any children?

(*They smile at each other. Hopelessly.*)

EROS: Your eyes have seen into the heart, the heart of love
          It was easier for baboons to adore the sun
          Than for you to look into the heart, the heart of love

(PHILIP *leaves*.)

          And now the vision is gone
          I do not control
          I offer a choice
          I say to your soul
          Rejoice!

(HALCY *and* PETER *return to* PENNY.)

HALCY: Look at the car drive away. It gets smaller and smaller
       and smaller and smaller . . .

PETER: Mommy had a white dress with a veil and white shoes and
       blue ribbons in her hair. Anything you want to know about
       Mommy's wedding, ask Peter. Yes, she did wear white.

(PENNY *holds* PETER *and* HALCY *to her.*

They sit. The children sleep in her lap.
Behind and over them, PHILIP *appears, angry, crowded with* KIDS.)

PHILIP: I sit in the plane. Me with how many kids in my lap look
out the window. I see these fingers pointing up into the sky.
Is that our dig?
A cloud passes and blocks my view.
The cloud appears to be in the shape of my first wife.
Another cloud in the shape of my university blocks the
view.
Another cloud in the shape of me prevents my seeing the
earth.
The attendant passes candy.
The kids are sobbing.
The coffin is in the hold with my son.
I see Mount Etna spewing out its lava.
The plane flies low over the volcano.
I see the blazing red flames below melting stones into liquid.
The pilot makes one circular passage around the crater, then
lifts up and vanishes into the night.

(*The lights fade on* PHILIP.
EROS *considers* PENNY *and* PETER *and* HALCY.)

EROS: At the end of a perfect day
          In Sicily
          Two people face the night in tragedy
          A boy dies
          A love dies
          A family dies
          But everything dies
          You know that
          They know that
          What's the big surprise?

          But look! what is that rising
          Over that hill?

It always has risen
It always will

So once more let it be spoken
The same tale spun
From out of the part of your soul that's not broken
Adore the Sun
Open your eyes
And Adore the Sun
Find your true god
And Adore the Sun
Sun!
Sun!
Sun!

(*The stage fills with blinding light.*
EROS *smiles over* PENNY *and the* TWO CHILDREN.
PENNY *looks up, eyes opened, into the light and makes that palms-up gesture.*)

END

SOMETHING
I'LL TELL YOU
TUESDAY

▲ ▲ ▲ ▲

SOMETHING I'LL TELL YOU TUESDAY was first presented by Joe Cino at the Caffe Cino, in New York City, on October 25, 1966. The director was Russ Kaiser, the lighting was by Donald Brooks, the Stage Manager was George Borris. The cast was as follows:

AGNES	Clio Vias
ANDREW	Frank Ammirati
HILDEGARDE	Sharkey Fink
GEORGE	John Fink
MRS. HASSELBACH	Joan Campbell

▲ ▲ ▲ ▲

The action of the play is the West 59th Street block between Eighth and Ninth avenues in New York City on a pleasant April day, first in a shabby brownstone walkup, then the corridor, the street, a lunch counter, and the street.

AGNES, *an old woman, sits packing a suitcase with nightgowns and a toothbrush and combs and brushes and curlers.*

ANDREW, *an old man, stands, back to her, staring out the window.*

AGNES: (*The tail end of a fight.*) If we left now, we could leave a note for them to meet us there.

ANDREW: They'll be here any minute.

AGNES: Andrew, it's only a block away—

ANDREW: It's a long block—

AGNES: It's such a nice day. Look at it outside. And I'll be flat on my back such a long time.

ANDREW: You'll only be there a couple of days. Doctor Daner said only a week maybe.

AGNES: Maybe, he said. I could be there a long time.

ANDREW: You won't be.

AGNES: Couldn't we walk? Oh, Andrew, I'll be flat on my back for God knows how long—

ANDREW: (*Turning to her.*) Don't say that—

AGNES: And I can rest. That's all I'll be doing is resting and—I'd like to walk with you. (*He looks at her. He takes his necktie off the back of the chair and begins tying it.*)

ANDREW: Well, I can't blame you for not wanting to drive with Hildegarde and George.

AGNES: (*Stops packing.*) Andrew?

ANDREW: Ah, it hurts me the way they fight. You all packed?

AGNES: (*Rises.*) You know what I was thinking about this morning? Come here—look at this. Look behind the picture.

ANDREW: What is it?

AGNES: Look behind the picture. (*He crosses up to her, pantomimes moving a picture away from the wall.*) Remember that?

ANDREW: (*Puzzled.*) What is it?

AGNES: That streak on the wall. Remember? (*She comes back down to her chair and resumes packing.*) The painters had just finished painting this room and the walls were still wet and we were fighting about something and I got mad at you and threw the grapefruit I was eating at you and you ducked and the grapefruit stuck to the wet wall and slid all the way down to the floor.

ANDREW: (*Pushing the picture back into place.*) That was a long time ago.

AGNES: I got up very early this morning. You were still asleep and I roamed around the apartment and I remembered why we hung that picture on the wall. I haven't thought of that in years.

ANDREW: (*Sharply.*) Are you all packed? (*He paces back and forth.*)

AGNES: I'm all ready. (*She hurries up packing and closes her bag.*)

ANDREW: I just wish this day were over.

AGNES: That's why I want to walk to the hospital. It'd be pleasant. We could leave a note for Hildegarde and George that we left already and they could meet us there. (HILDEGARDE *and* GEORGE *enter.* HILDEGARDE*'s hair is askew.* GEORGE *looks like he's on the brink of either murder or an ulcer.*)

GEORGE: Your mother's sick—for once in your life can't you think of somebody beside yourself—yatata yatata—

HILDEGARDE: (*Over the above.*) Don't get me started—don't get me started— (AGNES *and* ANDREW *hear them. They look at each other.* ANDREW *goes to answer the door. She pulls him back.*)

AGNES: (*Whispering.*) Andrew, don't answer the door. They'll think we've left and they'll go right to the hospital. We could take a cab if you're tired.

HILDEGARDE: (*Harshly.*) Oh for God's sake—shut up, George. (*Calling sweetly.*) Mama? Papa? Open up! We're here! Knock knock knock! (*She straightens her clothes and glares at* GEORGE.)

AGNES: (*Pleading, whsipering.*) Andrew, we haven't taken a walk together in so long. That's what I was thinking about this morning. Please, Andrew? (*His shoulders slump. He motions her to the door.*)

HILDEGARDE: (*Panic-stricken.*) You don't suppose anything's happened? Mama? Papa!

AGNES: Oh . . . (*Moving towards the door.*) We're here. Knock knock knock. Hello, Hildegarde. (*Pantomimes opening door.*) Hello, George. (HILDEGARDE *and* GEORGE *storm in.*)

ANDREW: Hello, Hildegarde. George.

HILDEGARDE: (*Quick kisses her parents.*) Well, why didn't you open? (GEORGE *sits.*) I have been so nervous today I'll expect anything. We have had THE worst trip in—

GEORGE: Just shut up, Hildegarde. We got here safe and just shut up. (ANDREW *starts off to get the coats.* AGNES *goes to pick up her bag.* HILDEGARDE *sits.* GEORGE *turns away disgustedly.*)

HILDEGARDE: Do we have time? I have just got to sit down and rest and catch my breath. (*She starts crying.* AGNES *comes and puts her hand around* HILDEGARDE's *shoulder.*)

GEORGE: For God's sake—it wasn't that bad.

HILDEGARDE: (*Furious.*) Oh, it's all right for you to talk—

GEORGE: (*Brightly, to his in-laws.*) Folks, we parked the car two blocks away. We were lucky. A DeSoto pulled out just as we came down the block, so anytime you're ready to leave, we'll go get it again.

HILDEGARDE: Just let me get my breath before we start out again.

GEORGE: We are just going down the block.

HILDEGARDE: (*Like it's the longest trip in the world.*) And then all the way back to Newark. I'm driving this time, George. You are not safe behind a wheel. (*Turning to her mother.*) Mama, he knocked over every one of those yellow markers on the George Washington Bridge.

GEORGE: I did not knock over every one of them. With you screaming at me. Agnes, you have a nice voice. Andrew, you have a nice voice. I do not know where she gets her voice from. She screams and it does something to your ears. (*Leans back disgusted.*) Ah, for God's sake, Hildegarde, let's not wash dirty linen in public.

HILDEGARDE: (*Horrified.*) This is not public. This is my home. This is the home I grew up in. (*She wraps her arms tightly around her mother's waist while she screams at* GEORGE.) He has no consideration. Every one of the yellow markers. I always thought they were metal, (*appealing to her mother*) so when he knocked them all over, naturally, I screamed.

GEORGE: (*All the hate in the world.*) They were only rubber, Hildegarde. Yellow rubber.

AGNES: (*Brightly, trying to get out of* HILDEGARDE*'s grasp.*) How are the children? (*She goes to her husband, rubbing her waist.*)

GEORGE: (*Glaring at* HILDEGARDE.) Fine.

HILDEGARDE: (*Murderously at* GEORGE.) We'll bring them over on Tuesday. It's a holiday in New Jersey.

ANDREW: (*Trying to break the tension.*) What's the holiday?

HILDEGARDE: Some tree day. (*Breaking down.*) Oh, mother, I would like to—

GEORGE: Don't start that crying again. (*He throws his hands up at his in-laws.*)

HILDEGARDE: (*Pulling together all her dignity.*) I would like to come to that hospital with you and just crawl in beside you and stay there. I'm so fed up. (*A whimper.*) So fed up.

GEORGE: (*Leaning forward to her.*) I wish you would stay in that hospital. And let me tell you one more thing. I knocked over all those yellow markers on purpose.

HILDEGARDE: (*Daring him.*) He's trying to drive me insane. Okay, George, drive me insane. If that's what's going to make you happy, you go right ahead and drive me insane. (GEORGE *stands up disgustedly.* HILDEGARDE *covers her head with her arms.*) Don't you dare hit me! (ANDREW *starts for her.* AGNES *pulls him back.*) Papa, help!

GEORGE: (*Amazed.*) I'm only going to get a glass of water. (*He exits shaking his head.* AGNES *takes* GEORGE*'s seat.*)

HILDEGARDE: (*Whispering to her mother.* ANDREW *comes over behind* AGNES *quickly to hear what she's saying.*) He called me the worst names once we got off that bridge. Names you wouldn't call the lowest scum on earth he called me. (AGNES *pats her hand.*)

GEORGE: (*Off.*) What're you saying?

HILDEGARDE: (*Whispering.*) He'd hit me. He has. He will.

GEORGE: (*Sticking his head out.*) Anybody want a glass of water or coffee or something?

HILDEGARDE: (*Offhand.*) I would like some water. Put sugar in it. (GEORGE *disappears back into the kitchen.* HILDEGARDE *pats her mother's hand with great dramatic concern.*) Oh, Mama, how are you? You're going to be all right. I said to George that DeSoto pulling out just as we came down the block is a good sign. You're going to be all right.

AGNES: (*Nobly.*) Don't be upset about me.

HILDEGARDE: Oh, it's not you, Mama. (AGNES *looks surprised.*) It's the kids. It's—it's him. It's everything. It's me. (*She starts laughing.*) Wow, aren't I the cheery one?

ANDREW: (*Touches her shoulder.*) Now that's the Hildegarde I like to see. (GEORGE *reenters with the sugared "glass of water."*)

GEORGE: (*Good-naturedly, to her.*) Minute I go out of the room she starts laughing.

HILDEGARDE: (*Still sore at him.*) Now don't try and make up.

GEORGE: (*Giving her the "glass."*) Maybe I should stay out of the room more often. (*He winks at* ANDREW. HILDEGARDE *sips.*)

AGNES: How's your water?

HILDEGARDE: (*Startled at first.*) What? Oh, this water. I thought you meant something else. This water—fine. Not as good as Jersey water—but still fine. (*Like a recipe.*) The sugar makes it sweet. (GEORGE *groans.*)

ANDREW: I think we should hurry. Hospitals run on a tight schedule.

HILDEGARDE: Oh, Papa, you're always in such a hurry. It's so nice here with you. (*Patting her mother's hand.*) My God, we won't always have this chance. (*Horrifying pause all around.* AGNES *goes to the window.*)

GEORGE: That's a rotten thing to say.

HILDEGARDE: (*Realizing what she's said.*) Mama, I didn't mean that. I meant—and this is the truth— (*Rises, goes to* AGNES.)—the way George drives, I don't know how many more chances we're going to get.

GEORGE: Just leave my driving out of it. Look at your father. He's quiet. He's happy. Why don't you take after him?

ANDREW: (*Sitting.*) I'm just thinking today, George. Just thinking.

HILDEGARDE: (*Laughing nervously.*) Thinking? About how you're going to be a bachelor while Mama's away? Mama, do you think you can trust him? (AGNES *smiles.*) That Mrs. Hasselbach on the third floor's always had her eye on Papa. Even when I was a little girl. (ANDREW *laughs at her. She goes to him, leans over from behind, and hugs him.*) It's the truth. I'd take the garbage down to the incinerator and Mrs. Hasselbach would stick her head out the door and she'd say, "Isn't your papa bringing the garbage to the incinerator today, dearie?"

AGNES: (*Playing along with* HILDEGARDE.) I think I can trust him.

ANDREW: (*Pushing* HILDEGARDE's *arms away.*) Of course you can.

HILDEGARDE: (*Happily, sitting.*) Papa, you're taking everything so seriously today. We're only teasing. Papa, Monica has her first date next Saturday. The High School Junior Prom. Isn't that nice? (GEORGE *comes behind* HILDEGARDE *and signals his in-laws not to get involved in this particular conversation.*)

ANDREW: (*Looking up at him, taking the cue.*) What? Oh, maybe we better get started— (*He starts to rise.*)

AGNES: (*Reaching for her suitcase.*) Yes, hospitals run on a—

HILDEGARDE: (*Turning to* GEORGE.) What's he doing? Oh, he doesn't want to talk about Monica. (*She stands up to him. He goes to her. She faces him.* AGNES *and* ANDREW *sigh and both sit down, exhausted.*) You don't want to talk about Monica. He knows he did wrong.

GEORGE: I did not do wrong. Your father probably did the same thing for you.

HILDEGARDE: He never did.

ANDREW: What's the matter? What wouldn't I do?

AGNES: Who's her date?

GEORGE: (*Proudly.*) Captain of the swimming team!

HILDEGARDE: Cocaptain of the swimming team. The way Monica talks about him you'd think he was Cary Grant or something. So George here goes out and buys her this fantastic evening gown.

GEORGE: (*Shuffling over by the window.*) It's her first big date.

HILDEGARDE: (*Pacing.*) It's cut down to here. She's only sixteen. She'll look like a freak. It wasn't even on sale. (AGNES *and* ANDREW *sit hypnotized—powerless—watching the fight between* HILDEGARDE *and* GEORGE *like a tennis match, their heads swinging right then left as* HILDEGARDE *and* GEORGE *shout back and forth.*)

GEORGE: So what? Your father probably did the same thing for you.

HILDEGARDE: Never! He never bought me a dress for more money than we could afford and my mother never had holes in her underwear. Mama, this sounds so crude to say—

GEORGE: Then don't say it!

HILDEGARDE: Here is Monica going to this dance. Only in the gymnasium. Wearing this fantastic evening gown that you can't even return. Now how can she have a good time knowing her mother is sitting up home waiting for her with holes in her underwear. Mama, all my lingerie is shot and here's Monica in this fantastic—cut down to here—it is just not fair!

GEORGE: Aha! (*Comes to her, mockingly.*) The truth comes out. You are a very jealous woman.

HILDEGARDE: (*Meeting him halfway.*) I AM NOT JEALOUS! And it's time we got started. I'm going to get the car. You all wait right here. I'll be back in a few minutes.

GEORGE: I'm driving the car.

HILDEGARDE: (*Holding out her hand.*) I will drive my parents to the hospital. You will give me the keys.

GEORGE: (*A warning in his voice.*) Hildegarde—

HILDEGARDE: (*Runs to her mother, hugging her, almost knocking her off the chair.*) Mama, he punched me. We got off that George Washington Bridge and he leaned over and punched me right in the side. I'm frightened of him, Mama.

GEORGE: I'll be right back with the car. Be waiting out front. (GEORGE *pantomimes opening the door, storms out down the dark corridor.* HILDEGARDE *runs to the door and screams down the corridor.*)

HILDEGARDE: Don't you dare leave without me. (*She turns to her parents, smiling nervously.*) I better go after him. You can't trust him alone. (*She comes to her mother and kneels in front of her, speaking to her like you would to a child.*) This is what I wanted to tell you. I'll bring the bed jacket on Tuesday. I went to buy it, but the salesgirl told me on the sly they're having this fantastic sale on them—the nice lacy ones—on Tuesday. So I'll bring the bed jacket then. Okay? (*She stands up, smiling.*) We'll be right back. We'll beep. (*Patting her mother's hand.*) And, Mama, don't worry! (*She leans over and kisses her father.*) Papa, she's going to be all right. (*She runs out the door down the corridor.*) George, if you step one foot in that

car, I swear you'll be sorry. (*And she is off.* AGNES *and* AN-
DREW *look at each other. They take a deep breath.* ANDREW *checks
his watch.*)

AGNES: Andrew?

ANDREW: (*Rubbing her knee.*) They'll be back in a few minutes.

AGNES: It'll take them about fifteen minutes, won't it? To get
back? Andrew, we could walk down the block in fifteen
minutes. Please, Andrew, it'd be like a date. Andrew, I don't
want to drive with Hildegarde and George.

ANDREW: Oh, I know what you mean there.

AGNES: (*Turning to him.*) And I'm not tired. I slept so well last
night and, Andrew, I'd just like to be alone with you.
Please? Are you tired?

ANDREW: Are you packed? (*She nods yes. He pauses.*) Then get
your coat on. (*He stands up.*) I'll leave a note. (*He pantomimes
writing a note. She runs off and returns with his coat and hat and
her coat and hat.*) I'll call a cab.

AGNES: No! I want to walk. (*She sticks her hat on. He takes his coat
from her and puts it on. He reaches over and helps her with hers.
She looks at him, surprised.*)

ANDREW: We better hurry. (*He picks up her suitcase. She buttons her
coat.* ANDREW *stands at the door. She looks around the apartment.*)
You'll be back next week . . .

AGNES: (*With infinite sadness.*) Yeah. Next week. (*She straightens
the two chairs, putting them side by side, stands behind them, then
goes out the door.* ANDREW *pantomimes closing the door. She
blocks his hand.*) Wait, Andrew . . . (*She looks in the doorway
through the apartment one more time, her eyes very wide. She
crosses out into the dark corridor.*) All right. (ANDREW *closes and
locks the door and sticks the note in the door. The light fades on the
apartment. The corridor where they are is lit. A head sticks out from*

a door: an old deaf lady in a too large robe she keeps wrapped around herself.)

MRS. HASSELBACH: (*Calling out.*) You leaving now?

AGNES: (*Calling up to her.*) Oh, hello, Mrs. Hasselbach. Yes, we're leaving now.

ANDREW: (*Tipping his hat embarrassedly.*) Hello, Mrs. Hasselbach.

MRS. HASSELBACH: I saw your daughter and son-in-law were here a few minutes ago.

AGNES: (*Loud, but pleasant.*) Yes. They came in from New Jersey.

MRS. HASSELBACH: (*Impressed.*) Oh, they live in New Jersey now? Nice. I have relations in New Jersey. Where do your daughter and son-in-law live in New Jersey?

AGNES: (*Happily.*) Well, nice seeing you, Mrs. Hasselbach. We better be going. All set, Andrew, Andrew? (*Loudly to her.*) Hospitals run on a tight schedule.

ANDREW: Nice seeing you, Mrs. Hasselbach.

MRS. HASSELBACH: I didn't notice any taxicabs waiting out front.

AGNES: We didn't call any taxicabs, Mrs. Hasselbach. We're walking.

MRS. HASSELBACH: (*Morbidly.*) On a day like this you're walking?

AGNES: It's a lovely day.

ANDREW: Don't let her think I'm a cheapskate.

AGNES: (*Laughing.*) And it's not because he's a cheapskate.

MRS. HASSELBACH: (*Offended.*) So who said?

ANDREW: Ask her to tell Hildegarde and George we left.

AGNES: (*Kidding coquettishly.*) Mrs. Hasselbach, Andrew has something to ask you.

MRS. HASSELBACH: (*Thrilled.*) Oooooo—what is it?

ANDREW: Thanks a lot, Agnes. (*Loud.*) Mrs. Hasselbach, when Hildegarde and George come back, would you tell them we left already? We left a note.

MRS. HASSELBACH: (*Musically.*) Certainly, Andrew. (*To* AGNES, *flat.*) I'll come visit you, dearie. Good luck. (*She exits.*)

ANDREW: (*A deep breath.*) Well, come on. Let's go . . . (*She opens the door and steps out into the street.*)

AGNES: (*Surprised.*) It's such a lovely day . . . such a pretty day . . . (*She takes his arm, looking all around her. He is troubled.*)

ANDREW: (*Stopping.*) Let me call a cab.

AGNES: (*Laughing.*) Look at her at the window up there behind the curtain. OooHoo! Hello, Mrs. Hasselbach.

ANDREW: (*Pulling her along.*) Now come on!

AGNES: (*As they walk.*) And the way she called you. Certainly, Andrew. You think I can trust you?

ANDREW: That's not funny.

AGNES: I'm only kidding. It's such a nice day.

ANDREW: (*Stopping again.*) Look, we just can't walk up to the hospital. Let me call a cab.

AGNES: Are you tired?

ANDREW: No.

AGNES: Is the suitcase heavy?

ANDREW: No.

AGNES: Then we'll walk. (*They begin walking the outer edge of the stage area in a clockwise direction. Her arm is wrapped tightly in his. Her eyes shine proudly, taking in everything around her. He looks morosely ahead.*)

ANDREW: (*Muttering.*) I don't want them thinking I'm a cheap-skate.

AGNES: Who? The hospital? Mrs. Hasselbach?

ANDREW: (*Pulling her sharply back.*) Watch out for that car— (*Follows the car till it's out of sight.*) Goddam drivers. (*They are at the curb. They step down in unison. They hurry across the street, looking both ways.*)

AGNES: (*As they cross the street.*) You were never what they call a John Jacob Astor, but you were never a Collier Brother either. People know you're no cheapskate.

ANDREW: Watch the sidewalk. (*They are at the curb, they step up in unison.*)

AGNES: You know why I want to walk? When we moved here forty years ago, I said it'll be good. Kids ever get sick, you ever get sick, Roosevelt Hospital is only a block away. We can walk. So in forty years, nobody ever gets sick enough to have to go to the hospital, except me now. So let me get something out of living here forty years. Let me walk to the hospital. (*Stops, gasps.*) Look what those kids wrote on the sidewalk. I don't think I ever learned that word till I was—

ANDREW: (*Sounding almost harsh.*) I don't think you ever learned that word. (*She looks at him, surprised for the second time today at him.*)

AGNES: That's— (*But they're at another crossing. He hurries her across the street to make the light. She stops him at the curb. They are both out of breath.*) That's very sweet.

ANDREW: (*Gruff.*) Way they change these lights before you get a chance to get across— Watch the curb. (*They step up in unison. They walk in silence till* AGNES *smiles.*)

AGNES: Remember the old *Fred Allen Show* on the radio about the house blew up and the old man and woman go flying through the sky and she says, "This is the first time we been out together in twenty years."

ANDREW: (*Laughing in spite of himself.*) Fred Allen was very funny.

AGNES: That's us. We haven't been out together like this in a very long while. This is like a date. I feel very young.

ANDREW: You are young.

AGNES: Listen, when your youngest daughter is having her change of life, you know you're not Shirley Temple anymore. (*Something catches her eye and she stops him.*) Andrew, could we have a cup of coffee?

ANDREW: We can't be late.

AGNES: You want to get rid of me?

ANDREW: NO! But—but hospitals run . . . let's get a cup of coffee. (*He sets down the suitcase. They sit on the chairs.* AN-DREW *holds up two fingers. They sit in silence, looking straight ahead. A moment later, they pantomime picking up their cups and begin sipping.* ANDREW *murmurs an automatic thank-you to the counterman.*)

AGNES: I always liked Bickford's coffee.

ANDREW: (*Frowning.*) Is Hildegarde having her change of—of life?

AGNES: (*Sipping.*) Ah, she'll be all right.

ANDREW: I wish they didn't fight so much—her and George.

AGNES: You know what I'm gonna tell her Tuesday when she comes with the kids? I was thinking this while I was watching them. I'm gonna tell her she's lucky they still fight. That's the worst part of getting old, I decided. You don't miss the love part, the sex part, the not being able to have kids part. You think that's the part you're gonna miss, but you know it's gonna go. No, the one thing I always thought we'd have, you and me, is the fights. God, didn't we toss some beautiful battles. And the neighbors hammering on the walls. (*Almost angry.*) Not even a hot bath or a cup of tea can make you feel as clean as when I'd finish yelling at you and you'd finish yelling at me. That's the worst part of getting old, I decided. You just don't have the energy to fight. (*A long pause.*)

ANDREW: We better go . . .

AGNES: (*Looking straight ahead, lost.*) Yeah . . . (*He throws two "dimes" on the counter. He stands up. He realizes he is old. He rises with great difficulty. She watches him, reaches for his hand, but needs both of her hands to lean forward on her knees to help herself rise. She takes his hand. He picks up the suitcase. They walk out very slowly. She stops him and looks at him. After a moment.*) God, Fred Allen was funny, wasn't he? (*They turn and walk out of sight.*)

END

THE LOVELIEST
AFTERNOON
OF THE YEAR

▲ ▲ ▲ ▲

THE LOVELIEST AFTERNOON OF THE YEAR was first presented by Joe Cino at the Caffe Cino, in New York City, on October 25, 1966. It was directed by Russ Kaiser with lighting by Donald Brooks and scenery by John Guare. The Stage Manager was George Borris. The cast was as follows:

SHE   Karlene Weise
HE   Frank O'Brien

▲　▲　▲　▲

Calliope music plays and fades as the curtain rises.
A shy young girl sits feeding pigeons in the park for want of anything
better to do.
Autumn day. Crisp air: The kind called invigorating.
A young man enters in a panic, sees her, gasps.

HE: I wish you wouldn't feed the pigeons! (SHE *freezes.*) Please.
　　I wish you wouldn't feed the pigeons . . .

SHE: (*Looking at him.*) Huh?

HE: I wouldn't mind you feeding—

SHE: (*Stands up, clutching her purse.*) Are you a mugger?

HE: —the pigeons— No! I'm not a mugger. I'm just trying to
　　tell you—

SHE: (*Petrified.*) Because if you are a mugger, I'll scream. I'll have
　　those cops after you so quick—

HE: I am trying to tell you—

SHE: (*A warning whisper.*) I love to scream. I have a very loud
　　voice.

HE: I don't believe that.

SHE: (*Rummaging in her purse.*) Where is my tear gas gun?

HE: (*Terror-stricken.*) I don't want you feeding pigeons because I
　　just saw pigeons at the Seventy-ninth Street Entrance and
　　the covey of them—the whole bunch of them—whatever

you call a bunch of pigeons—a gaggle—all those pigeons had *foam*— (SHE *stops rummaging through her purse.*) were foaming at the mouths.

SHE: (*Simply.*) I'll scream.

HE: At the *beaks*? Pigeons were foaming at the beaks—all of them.

SHE: Who the hell are you?

HE: (*Pleading.*) I'm very hungry and hate to see you feeding pigeons when I'm hungry. A Cracker Jack at this point would be a feast. (HE *goes to her.* SHE *moves away.*)

SHE: I don't believe you.

HE: (*Sits down dejectedly on bench.*) You're very perceptive. I— actually, it's the birthday of this child and I promised this child a present and I know at the bottom of that box *is* a present and (*seductively*) I was wondering if you'd let me have it. (SHE*'s shocked.* SHE *swings her bag at him.* HE *ducks to protect himself.*) The present! The little plastic present . . .

SHE: Buddy, I bet you got more money in the silk change pocket of that fancy sport coat of yours than I got in my whole imitation alligator bag.

HE: (*Stands up, desperate.*) That's not true! My wife takes all my money and she bends it in her teeth so I can't use it. I have to walk everywhere because she bends all my subway tokens. And she has a blue rifle with a silencer on it and shoots my feet so I have to dance this crazy darting dance whenever I come in late. (HE *stares at her in desperation. Her jaundiced eye grows curiouser and curiouser. A moment of silence.* SHE *bursts out laughing and hands him the Cracker Jack.*) Please? Believe me? Everything I say is true. Please don't laugh. (SHE *is so happy.* HE *eats Cracker Jacks nervously.* HE *finds a plastic ring in the box.* SHE *turns to him.*)

SHE: I have been in this city eleven months now and you are the first person I've spoken to. That's spoken to me. Eleven months of silence—till now. I feel like I've just been released from a convent—a goddam convent. No, I'm not laughing at you. I'm a young girl and I'm pretty and nobody ever speaks to me—not even to ask directions—and you're the funniest man I've ever met and I thank you in all the languages there are. Thank you for speaking to me.

HE: Everything I've said is true! (HE *turns to go.* SHE *touches his arm.*)

SHE: Oh God—please? Don't leave. (HE *turns to her. They look at each other.* HE *puts the Cracker Jack under the bench and slips the plastic ring on her finger.* SHE *looks at it. Then at him. A shy kiss that turns into a long kiss. Then they both turn joyously to us in the audience.*)

HE: (*To us.*) And that's how we met two Sundays ago. And we walk in the park. This is the third Sunday we've met now. We talk about the future . . . (*They walk in place, their arms locked. They are lovers. They talk to the audience.*)

SHE: It's autumn and orange and green and blue and yellow leaves are all over the ground and our feet make a scuffing noise like this . . . chh chh chh . . .

HE: And when we get home, our socks have orange and green and blue and yellow leaf shreds in them stuck in the wool.

SHE: Now wait—his socks and his home. I wear nylons and I have my apartment and he doesn't know where I live and I don't know where he lives. He has his life and I have mine.

HE: Except for Sunday. Today. We walk along and talk about the future. We never mention the past. And our feet make a scuffing noise like this . . . chh chh chh . . .

SHE: Now wait, just because we don't talk about the past, don't get the idea I'm any slut or something. I'm just an Ohio girl.

O-H-Ten. You only talk about the past when you have a past. (*Embarrassed smile.*) I must remember not to wear this sweater any more Sundays.

HE: I think she still thinks I'm a mugger.

SHE: I spent all last Monday picking these long shreds of dead grass out of the back of my sweater with a silver tweezer. Oh, I don't care if he's a mugger or not!!! I'm not going to take any chances, no siree, like meeting him at night or during the week when there's nobody around. But Sundays are okay—and, mugger or not—I like him very much. He's really an odd person—an odd duck. But he does tell me awfully funny stories. (*To him, shyly.*) Hey, tell me a funny story?

HE: They're not funny stories. They're true!

SHE: (*To us.*) True! Listen to this one, please. We're in the Zoo near the polar bear cage. Now I have never seen a polar bear. (*Excited.*) Hey, look at the polar bear! (SHE *reaches out to touch it through the bars.*)

HE: (*Violently pulling her back.*) Don't do that!!!!

SHE: I never saw a polar bear, for God's sake. It won't kill me.

HE: Won't kill you! Listen, ten years ago, my sister Lucy was a top debutante—

SHE: (*Impressed.*) Really?

HE: And after her coming-out party at the Hotel Plaza back there, Lucy and her two escorts broke into this part of the Zoo and Lucy stuck her arm into this cage—this very cage—just as you did now before I stopped you. And this polar bear—(HE *follows the polar bear with an accusing finger, shakes it three times.*) No, I don't think it was *this* polar bear—this one doesn't look familiar— (SHE *comes to him.*) But the polar bear—the one ten years ago—bit my sister Lucy's arm right off at the *breast!* (HE *turns away, covering his face.*)

SHE: OMIGOD!

HE: And we heard her screams clear over to the Plaza and the doctors came and (*petulant*) we all had to leave the coming-out party. I was very young—well, eighteen—

SHE: What did they do?

HE: My parents shrieked, "Do something, do something," and the doctors and all the ambulances which came (*pantomimes dramatically*) pulled Lucy's arm out of the polar bear's mouth and quickly sewed it back on. Modern surgery can do things like that.

SHE: (*Truly horrified.*) What happened?—Omigod!!!!

HE: The arm grew back—thank God—but Lucy never went to another coming-out party again.

SHE: Boy, I can see why not.

HE: Because enormous amounts of—she developed all over her body—enormous amounts of white polar bear hair and for her comfort we had to ship her to Alaska in a cage.

SHE: (*Suspicious.*) You're putting me on.

HE: (*Disparaging her disbelief.*) You're from Ohio. You come from a nice little family. You don't understand the weirdness, the grief that people can spring from—

SHE: You're the oddest duck I have ever met.

HE: (*Horrified.*) Ducks! You stay away from ducks. I can tell you a story about my aunt—

SHE: (*Hands over her ears.*) Please. I don't want to hear any more stories. We said we'd just talk about the future.

HE: The future! If you came from a past like I have—such as mine—the idea of riding—galloping into a future which would ultimately turn into past (*turns to her accusingly*) would make you break out in hives and your hair would fall out.

SHE: (*Backs away from him.*) Well, it won't fall out and if you keep on talking like that, I'll go home and wash it and massage it and make sure—damn good and sure—that it doesn't fall out. (HE *is hurt.*) So let's just walk in silence and— (SHE *extends her hand.* HE *takes it. They turn and walk in place. They smile at each other, remembering they are lovers.*) Listen, do you hear that merry-go-round! I always like calliope music. Isn't that what they call it?

HE: Yes. They run on steam. My father fell in one and was scalded to death.

SHE: (*Stops walking.*) Please . . . let's just walk and sing. (*They stroll arm in arm. The tune is "Over the Waves." They both hum as they stroll.*) Do you really have a wife?

HE: (*Fingers to his lips.*) Shhhhh . . . (HE *smiles peacefully.*)

SHE: (*Over his humming.*) That's one story you told me I wonder if it's true. You told me your wife had a blue rifle with a silencer on it and shot you in the feet if you came in late. You told me that three weeks ago. I hope you don't have a wife. I'd hate it if you had a wife.

HE: Since I met you, I don't have a wife.

SHE: Are you divorced?

HE: (*Looking straight ahead.*) No.

SHE: But you do have a wife?

HE: (*Beat.*) No.

SHE: (*Laughing, snuggling up to him.*) At least not a wife who carries a blue rifle and shoots you if you come in late.

HE: (*Stops their walking and turns to her desperately.*) I have no wife. Listen, since I met you—these last three Sundays—the last three weeks have had music. I don't mean all violins and trombones. I mean I've been conscious of the rhythm in people's walking, the music in the turning of the turnstiles in the subway at rush hour.

SHE: (*Pulling his hands away.*) I thought you said your wife bent your subway tokens so you couldn't go anywhere.

HE: (*Angry.*) I don't have a wife and I sneak under the turnstiles. You've saved my life. I've never picked anybody else up before but something about you—the way you fed those pigeons—I wanted to know you, and now . . . now it looks like I'd better thank you. (SHE *smiles, puzzled.* HE *sits her on the bench and kneels in front of her.* HE *begins to sing loudly and sweetly to her to the tune of "Over the Waves."*)

     You knelt and you fed
     Little pigeons sweet pieces of bread

(SHE *takes a long embarrassed look out to the audience.* HE *continues singing.*)

     Those pigeons could kill
     Or at least make you feel very ill

SHE: (*Then, to him, over his singing.*) What do you mean—thanking me? Is this the last time? Aren't I going to see you anymore? (*Fiercely.*) Don't *sing* so loud!

HE: (*Lost in the romance of his song.*)
     We saved both our lives
     Which should lead to husbands and wives

SHE: (*Total embarrassment.*) People are staring at you! Please, tell me—why are you thanking me? (HE'*s lost in his song.* SHE *beats him on the chest to get his attention.*)

HE: But since we must part
        Feed the pigeon that cries in my heart

SHE: (*Stands up. Walks behind the bench and faces him.*) Are you leaving me?

HE: Pigeons that (*changes key three tones higher*) cry in my heart!

(HE *stops singing suddenly.* HE *stands up. Pause. Quietly.*) I can't marry you. I can't see you during the week. I owe you something at least for all the music. Maybe we could meet a few times during the year. Bump into each other? (SHE *moves away, deeply hurt.*) Do you like that song?

SHE: I don't give a damn about that song.

HE: (*Comes up behind her.*) Do you know who sang that song?

SHE: I don't care who sang that song.

HE: Mario Lanza . . . and right after he sang it, he grew very fat and died. And then a few months later, his wife took drugs and she died too. Now that's true. You can read that in the newspapers.

SHE: So it's all off . . .

HE: Do you know what my job is? I've never told you.

SHE: So I'll spend the rest of my life feeding pigeons in the park. Maybe I'll meet somebody else . . .

HE: I'm a seeing-eye person for blind dogs. And that's very ironic. Because you've made me see so many things—to hear music in those subway turnstiles at rush hour . . .

SHE: (*Seeing something in the distance.*) Maybe it's just as well . . .

HE: And I've made you see nothing. (HE *turns away.*)

SHE: I want to be married. I like you. I'd like to be married to you . . . but I see people like her over there—that incredibly fat woman pushing those two—yes, two—incredibly fat children in that bright blue perambulator with that dog on the leash, and I say what's the use of being married. It obviously didn't make her happy . . . what's the good of marriage?

HE: (*Turning back to her and peering over her shoulder, holding his breath.*) What incredibly fat woman?

SHE: You can't see her now. She just passed behind that rock. Why fall in love with anybody? You just get hurt. I'm young. I'm pretty. I don't need anybody. (HE *suddenly crouches down behind her, holding her legs, peeking out from around her hips*.) What are you doing?

HE: That woman—what did you say she was pushing?

SHE: (*Annoyed*.) A bright blue perambulator with two enormous young . . . (*shocked*) that's—that's your wife, isn't it? You weren't fooling . . .

HE: (*petrified*.) And what did you say she had on a leash?

SHE: (*Squinting to see them in the distance*.) A dog . . . a great Great Dane and look—it just bumped its head into that tree and she yanks it back and it falls down against a bench.

HE: The dog has no eyes, has it?

SHE: The dog has no eyes and the children are so ugly and your wife—you have to go home to that every night? (HE *stands up and crosses to the bench*.)

HE: We work together. Dogs that can see bite her. (HE *sits down on the bench, back to audience*.) Oh, I can't divorce her. You can divorce a pretty wife for a homely one, but you can't switch an ugly one for a beautiful one. (SHE *walks to him slowly and faces him hesitantly*.)

SHE: Am I beautiful?

HE: You're very beautiful.

SHE: I really love you.

HE: (*Pulls her down beside him*.) Don't let her see us. Under those two babies, she carries the blue rifle with the silencer on it. She'd shoot us if she saw us together.

SHE: And would that be any worse than you leaving me, me leaving you, you going back to her, me going back to my empty apartment? (SHE *turns away from him.*) The last tenant left hundreds of murder mysteries and I'm afraid to read them. (HE *turns her to him.*)

HE: My wife's name is Maud. I'm going to call her. (HE *kisses her. He stands up, calling.*) Maud?

SHE: (*Stands beside him, calls quietly.*) Hey, Maud?

HE: (*Louder.*) Maud? Maud!

SHE: (*Louder.*) Hey, Maud!!!!

HE: (*Happily.*) She sees us! She's seen us! Hey, Maud! (SHE *kisses him all over his face so Maud will see, all the time they both keep waving and jumping up and down.*)

SHE: (*Suddenly shocked.*) Look! She's lifting the babies out and throwing them on the ground!

HE: The dog rears up and here comes the blue rifle. Hang on. (SHE *is shot by the rifle with the silencer.* SHE *clutches her stomach in amazement.* HE *is shot. They fall onto the bench, leaning over it, their knees almost on the ground.*)

SHE: (*Tapping him on the shoulder.*) Hey, you really do have a sister Lucy, don't you?

HE: (*In pain.*) I do. (*They reach for each other, but both fall dead on either side of the bench.*)

END

A DAY
FOR SURPRISES

▲ ▲ ▲ ▲

A DAY FOR SURPRISES was first presented in August of 1967 at the Caffe Cino, in New York City. The director was Bernie Wagner.

The play was also included in *The Best Short Plays 1970,* edited by Stanley Richards.

CHARACTERS

A	Virginia Blue
B	Robert Frink

Scene:	The pasting room of a very large library.
Time:	The present.

At curtain, B *is pasting books. Peace. A Vivaldi runs through his head: Autumn. The door bursts open.* A *staggers in: Sacré du Printemps. His stern look makes her straighten into, shape up into the formality he demands of a subordinate.*

A: (*A gasp.*) Pppppppardon me, Sir—bbbbbbbbut you have got HAVE GOT to llllloooook out your window—

B: (*With great distaste.*) Your paste pot is dried up.

A: Sir, you have got to look out—

B: (*Pasting, muttering.*) Less time picking up coffee nerves on coffee breaks, more time collecting overdue fines, we might have more of a library— (*She collapses on her chair in a paroxysm of hysteria.*)

A: Mr. Falanzano, you have got to look out your window—

B: (*Pasting, laughing.*) And you used up your two-week vacation? Frazzle frazzle frazzle. Another nightmare year in the overdue fine room.

A: SIR!

B: (*Exasperation.*) All right all right. (*He looks out the window. First left. Then right. He collapses.*)

A: (*A last bid for sanity.*) Tell me what you see—

B: (*Aghast.*) It's what—what I don't see—

A: What don't you see????

B: The lion—the lion closest to Forty-second Street—

A: Yes? Yes?

B: (*Grabbing up the phone.*) Operator, operator. (*No response.*) The lion closest to (*click click click*) to Forty-second Street is—

A: (*Putting the phone down.*) It's missing, isn't it?

B: The stone lion is missing.

A: (*She is calm now.*) I know where it is.

B: That stone lion weighs 28,000 pounds . . .

A: I know where the stone lion is. (*He looks up at her. Her knowledge stabs her with pain again. Quietly.*) The stone lion is in—I assume it's the same one— There's a lion in the Ladies' Room and it's *eaten* Miss Pringle. (*His hands fly to his face.*) It's sitting in the Ladies' Room with Miss Pringle's feet sticking out of its mouth—out of the lion's mouth. I know it's Miss Pringle as I'd been admiring her blue beaded shoes only this morning and the way she braided the hair on her legs into the new black lacy stockings. The lion's on its haunches right by the washstand just the way it sits out front—only . . . only Miss Pringle's feet are sticking out its mouth . . .
I ran out of this library screaming—I ran right out onto Fifth Avenue and when I saw the lion closest to Forty-second Street was not there—was absent—was A.W.O.L.—I thought I had gone insane—thought I had snapped! All this library paste. Kids sniff this stuff! I thought it had got to me—but you see it too! I'm not alone! Oh God, thank you, Mr. Falanzano! Thank God for you . . . (*She hugs him. She is calmed. She hangs on to him. He raises his head. His face is a pitiful sight.*)

B: It's eaten Miss Pringle? (*He leaps up and runs out of the room to the ladies' room.*)

A: You stay out of there! That's No Man's Land! (*He returns with a pair of blue beaded shoes.* A, *chiding:*) You peeked into No Man's Land. (*She is sufficiently calmed to return to work. She begins pasting books with a certain flair that only peace can bring.*) No need to worry really. (*She thumbs rapidly through an encyclopedia.*) It says here—L L L L L L L L Linnaeum Linoleum *Lion*—Lion: "after devouring prey, are satiated for two to three weeks." We're safe, Mr. Falanzano—for another couple of weeks anyway—

B: (*Glassy-eyed.*) Miss Jepson, I loved Miss Pringle.

A: I liked her too, for God's sake, but let's not get all soppy-eyed sentimental—

B: Miss Pringle and I were going to—to be married . . . (*He looks at the shoes, then throws his head down on the desk. He weeps. She is shocked by this disclosure, but quickly recovers.*)

A: Well, you sneakies! You and Miss Pringle! Why don't you let anybody *know!* Isn't this a day for surprises! You and Denise Pringle— It's like all the surprises of the world store themselves up for a day when the one thing you do not need is a surp . . . you and Denise Pring . . . sonofagun . . . like today . . . who needs a surprise today? I was going to go home, curl up with a good book, like any other night—look at the phone and welcome even a Sorry Wrong Number . . . Guiltily turn on my TV and watch reruns of beautiful domestic comedies—*Father Knows Best*—*Make Room for Daddy*—hi, Lucy, Hi, Doris! Then turn them off because it's time to water my geranium. But today will give me something to think about . . . a day for surprises . . . you and Miss Pringle . . .

B: Me and Miss Pringle . . . (*She touches his shoulder comfortingly. He pats her hand. A lion growls ferociously outside the door. They look up. They hold each other. The lion growls fiercely. The lion burps.*)

A: Would you like to come over to my place tonight?

B: (*Listening for the lion.*) Shhhhhhhh—

A: (*Seductively.*) Check over some books—

B: (*Uncomfortably.*) There's a lion outside the door—

A: (*Snuggling.*) Start something between the covers?

B: (*Breaking the embrace.*) Miss Jepson, my fiancée is DEAD!

A: What do you want me to do? Start pasting Denise Pringle memorial stickers in front of all the *Britannicas*? I'll do it, but I'm not going to waste my youth weeping over a not-very-attractive girl who was hardly worthy of you. Life has handed us a surprise! There's so few surprises that I want to leap at the present life has given me—you feel so nice—I want to leap before the lion eats me . . . those blue beaded shoes . . . that's not the first time the Lion came into the Ladies' Room and eaten one of the staff. Remember Miss Ramirez?

B: And nobody reports these horrors???????

A: There's a lot of lonely girls in this town, Mr. Falanzano. You know what the biggest lie is? The more the merrier.

B: (*A long pause . . .*) I . . . don't . . . under . . . unders . . .

A: (*Petting him.*) Shhhhh . . . shhhhhh . . . comfort . . . comfort . . .

B: . . . understand . . .

A: I'll sing you a song . . . a song by Sir Alfred Lord Tennyson . . . yes . . . you'll like that . . . (*Sings softly:*) Charles gave Elizabeth a dodo.

B: (*Pulling away.*) Books . . . poets . . . Alfred Lord Tennyson . . . I don't want to hear about books!! (*He has a fit and rips all the books in the room in pieces. She tries to restrain him. He sits*

in the wreckage of the books, and pieces of paper fall down on him.
He is angry and mad, and she is petrified. He fingers the cover of
a book. His voice is cold and repressed and tight.) My whole
world was books, Miss Jepson. It always has been. Until.
Until. One night . . . I came back late to the library because
I couldn't sleep and wanted a book—needed a book—
demanded the company of a volume. And I heard whimpering from the stacks . . . There was Miss Pringle whom I
didn't even know had a pass key—whom I'd never spoken
to—even when we met at clearance sales at Marboro Books
. . . there was Miss Pringle, whimpering and holding
volumes of Lewis Carroll, Camus, Proust, the *Joy of Cooking,*
holding these volumes and weeping . . . the overdue cards
in the back of the books slipping out like tears that piled up
around her ankles, then her knees. I called out: "Miss Pringle!" She stopped and sniffed like a suddenly spied gazelle in
some tropical quiet place. "Who is it?" she called out across
the black library. "Who is that? I have spent twenty years of
my precious life in school and I have just signed up for
courses in the fall. If I don't become a member of the human
race soon, I'll kill myself. Who is that? Is that you, Mr.
Falanzano? Please love me. I'm here. I'm ready." And we
raced to each other and the wind our two bodies made
racing—running to each other—set all the overdue cards
flying into the air—overdue cards no longer, but blossoms
from a thank-God early Spring. Her plea for help had
sounded an echo—a Little Sir Echo from my own heart, and
I quickly undressed her and then myself and then—while
she arranged our things with the neatness that was her trademark and the bane of the overdue fine room, I arranged on
the floor of the Neglected Masterpieces Section, a bed—a
couch made of photostats of Elizabethan Love Lyrics. She
said I've never loved anybody so I want this to be good. I
said oh, I had never loved anybody before either. So I took
a copy of *Love Without Fear* and she took a Modern Manual
on How to Do It, and we wrapped—like Christmas pack-

ages for people you love—wrapped our bodies, our phos-
phorescent, glowing, about-to-become-human bodies
around each other. And began reading. For the first time in
our lives, we wore flesh for clothing instead of baggy tweed.
After many months of this meeting at night in the stacks,
undressing, reading all the books on the Art and Science of
Love—boning up you might say for our final exam—after
many months of this study, we felt we had the system down:
Up. In. Oh oh oh. We had written that formula down many
times to make sure we knew it by rote. In the world of sex,
you want nothing to go wrong. I bought contraceptives and
she bought contraceptives as we had been instructed to do
in the *New York Post*'s weekend series: *Stop That Baby,* and
we finally felt we were ready. There was a full moon that
night. We took a quick gander at *Human Sexual Response*
and cleared our throats. The library closed and we came out
of our hiding places after the watchmen passed by and met
in the stacks of—The Rare Book Room! To be double sure,
she had wrapped herself in Saran Wrap from head to toe and
I remembered the lessons I had been taught and pinned the
Playmate of the Month over her head and finally proceeded
into her. Perhaps some of the one hundred and twenty-
seven rubber devices I wore on my erect bookmark dulled
some of the sensation. But I must say all went well—as well
as Chapter Seven of *Ideal Marriage* and a pamphlet from the
U.S. Government Printing Office had led us to believe. If
we had been doing it for credit, I would have given us an
A. An A plus! Well, a B plus anyway. A few weeks later,
Miss Pringle came to me with tears in her eyes. You were
having a coffee break. Tears in her watermark blue eyes. She
stood me right here and placed my pasting hand on her
womb. I felt a swelling. A distension. Life? Within her?
Somehow, despite the one hundred and twenty-seven suits
of armor, the eleven diaphragms, the six hundred and
eighty-two white pills, the three one-hundred-foot rolls of
Saran Wrap, despite all these precautions, somehow life had

managed to creep—no, triumph through! I loved Miss Pringle! She did not want the child. We took a book from the
uptown—the Yorkville Branch, where nobody knew us.
We took out Ann Landers's *Getting Rid of that Senior Prom
Boo-Boo and Put Yourself into Freshman Honors.* It contained
all the information, technical and otherwise, that we needed
for getting rid of our child. What had been our photostatic
bed of love became an operating table and I remember
seeing through her legs the photostat of a poem by Sir Philip
Sidney: "Ring out your bells / Let mourning shows be
spread / For love is dead . . ." And I who had been so proud
of myself for inserting life into a difficult envelope, proceeded again into Miss Pringle and removed—not a child—
not a miniature fetus of me . . . I removed—my hands felt
it and pulled out a small undeveloped volume of the Complete Works of Doctor Spock. Only *this* big—time
would've gestated it into a full set—time and nature . . . but
what hurt me was my—juice of which I'd been so proud—
hubristically proud for leaping so many hurdles like a Kentucky Derby Day dark-horse winner—no, an Olympic
runner who finally carries that Torch of Life and plants it in
the very summit of Mount Olympus to claim it for himself—that juice I bragged to call triumphant could only
father—only create a dull set of books. The flour and water
of library paste. Not semen at all. My life has been lived in
books. I had become a book . . . Library paste . . . we all
would've been better off if we'd never opened a book
. . . (*Long pause. She begins pasting him with paste from the paste
pot. She pastes her hand to his cheek. She pastes his hand to her
breast. She looks over his shoulder out the window.*)

A: Look . . . The lion's walking down the steps back to its perch.
Isn't that New York for you? Nobody even looks. They all
think it's *Candid Camera.* You could strut down Fifth Avenue N.U.D.E. and nobody'd even look . . . I mean, I'd look
at you, Mr. Falanzano, with your clothes on or anything

. . . (*She is at peace and crying and happy. They are beginning to cry onto each other.*) The lion's on its perch now. You'd never even know he moved. Except for that little piece of pink garter on its tooth dangling like a salmon . . . you'd never even know he moved . . .

B: You'd never even know he moved . . . (*They hold each other.*)

A: A day for such surprises . . . (*She strokes his hair and sings softly:*)
"Charles gave Elizabeth a dodo
And he never even offered one to me
A lovely lemon colored dodo
With eyes as green as grass could be.
Now it isn't that I'm doubting that Charles loves me
For I know that he would take me out to tea
But he did give Elizabeth a dodo
And he never even offered one to me."

(*The lights dim slowly.*)

CURTAIN

MUZEEKA

▲ ▲ ▲ ▲

MUZEEKA was given its first New York performance at the Provincetown Playhouse, on April 28, 1968. It was directed by Melvin Bernhardt and designed by Peter Harvey, and produced by Betty Ann Besch and Warren Lyons. The sound was by James Reichert and the lighting by Johnny Dodd. The stage movement was by Ralf Harmer. The cast was as follows:

JACK ARGUE	Sam Waterston
HIS WIFE	Marcia Jean Kurtz
EVELYN LANDIS	Peggy Pope
NUMBER TWO	Sandy Baron
STAGEHANDS	Kevin Brian Conway, John Lawlor, Frank Prendergast

Prior to the New York production, the play was first performed at the Eugene O'Neill Memorial Theatre Foundation in Waterford, Connecticut, on July 19, 1967. The players were Charles Kimbrough, Peggy Pope, Michael Douglas, William Rhys, and Linda Segal, and it was directed by Melvin Bernhardt. The play was subsequently performed at the Mark Taper Forum in Los Angeles, on October 10, 1967. The players were Philip Proctor, Sheree North, Philip Austin, and Caroline MacWilliams. It was produced by Gordon Davidson and directed by Edward Parone.

▲ ▲ ▲ ▲

Scene One

The STAGEHANDS *carry across an enormous banner, as they will at the beginning of each scene. It reads:*

"IN WHICH ARGUE SINGS THE PENNY."

ARGUE *is sitting on the edge of the lower bunk.*

ARGUE (*sings*):
     United States of America
     E Pluribus Unum
     O
     N
     E
(*Speaks:*) Cent (*Turns coin over. Sings:*)
     In God We Trust
     L
     I
     B
     Eeeeeee
     R
     Teeeeee
     Y
(*Speaks:*) 1965.

     Flips coin.
     He makes a choice.
     Uncovers coin.
     He stands up, beaming.

ARGUE: Heads!

(*Blackout*)

Scene Two

"IN WHICH ARGUE SAYS 'I LOVE YOU.'"

ARGUE *and his* WIFE *are in the lower bunk making love. He smiles at her and touches her face.*

ARGUE: I love you.

(*Blackout*)

(*Argue's* WIFE *is furiously turning the pages of a magazine.*)

ARGUE (*desperate*): I love you.

(*Blackout*)

(ARGUE *sits up reading* Playboy *magazine. His* WIFE *is sobbing.*)

ARGUE (*blandly*): I love you.

(*Blackout*)

Scene Three

"IN WHICH ARGUE HAS A VISION."

ARGUE *sits on the edge of the lower bunk. His* WIFE, *lying in the lower bunk covered by a sheet, watches him, one arm over her head, one eye showing, watching.*

ARGUE: If I could've been born anybody—my pick of a Kennedy or a Frank Sinatra or a Ford or the King of Greece—out of that whole hat of births, I still would've picked to be an Etruscan. Nobody knows where they came from. The archaeologists guess maybe they were one of the first tribes of Rome about a million years ago when Romulus and Remus

were posing for that Roman statue—that baby picture—of
them suckling life from a wolf. Well, Romulus and Uncle
Remus must've hoarded all that wolf milk to themselves
because the Etruscans vanished without a trace, like a high,
curved wave that breaks on the sand and retreats right back
into the sea. Vanished. Poof. Splash.

And the only footprints the Etruscans left behind were
these jugs. These jugs and pots and bottles and urns covered with pictures. Line drawings much like Picasso's.
The whole world can sue me for libel but I accuse Pablo
Picasso of stealing all his line drawings from the Etruscans.
J'accuse! J'accuse Pablo Picasso! Pots and jugs covered
with people dancing. ALL dancing. Warriors dancing.
Men dancing. Women dancing. Servants dancing. Prosti-
tutes dancing. Old men with bottles of wine and they're
dancing. A whole civilization dancing. Every part of them
dancing. Not just their feet, but their hands and heads and
beards and peckers and bosoms and shoulders and noses
and toes all dancing. And these smiles—these lovely,
loony smiles—that should make them look like a race of
Alfred E. Neumans except only genius could know the
joy that's painted on those pots and bottles and urns. All
painted in earth colors: blacks and browns and tans and
white. A whole civilization danced up out of the earth.
Danced up out of the ground all over the ground and
vanished. Maybe they just danced right into the pots and
what we see being held prisoner in museums is not line
drawings of Etruscans, but the Etruscans themselves,
dancing right inside the pots. If I could've been born anybody in the world ever—a Kennedy or Sinatra or Henry
Ford or the King of Greece—I still would've picked out
of that whole hat of births, picked Etruscan.

I'm going to take the job with Muzeeka, Sally-Jane.

(*He stands up and pulls on trousers and slips an already tied necktie over
his head.*)

(*Three* STAGEHANDS *come forward. I assumes a chairlike position. 2 sits on him as the Boss. 3 kneels on all fours.* ARGUE *sits on him.*)

ARGUE (*earnestly, suavely, to the Boss*): I can't compose, but I can arrange and, Sir, I want to be with the biggest largest piped-in music company in the whole wide world, so I'm picking the Muzeeka Corporation of America International over all the record companies and movie studios I've had offers from.

(*The Boss thinks a very long moment.* ARGUE *leans forward in suspense. The Boss stands up, beaming. He shakes hands with* ARGUE. ARGUE *pumps his hand with both hands and turns to us.*)

I'm in! I'm in!

(*Muzak plays, blandly. The three* STAGEHANDS *sit cross-legged in a row and pantomime playing violins and horns.* ARGUE *conducts them but talks over his shoulder to us.*)

ARGUE (*to us*): I'll start first with the violins. The Old Give 'Em What They Want. I'll wait with my tongue in my cheek here like a private smirking soul-kiss and when I'm piped into every elevator, every office, every escalator, every toilet, every home, airplane, bus, truck, and car in this country, I'll strike.

(*The* STAGEHANDS *fade away.* ARGUE *turns full to us.*)

Do you know about the cortical overlay that covers fifty percent of the human brain, deadening all our instincts so we have to be given lessons in every facet of living—except dying, of course. The human and the dolphin are the only animals that have this clay pot on the brain How the dolphins manage to survive, I can't figure out. But they'll have to take care of themselves. I'm involved with the humans.

I'll wait till all humans are inured to the ever-present, inescapable background ocean blandness of my music, till everyone knows down deep I'll always be there, stroking that cortical overlay till it's as hard and brittle as the clay of an

Etruscan pot and then, on a sudden day that is not especially
spring, not especially summer, a day when the most exciting
thing around is the new issue of the *Reader's Digest,* and you
read with interest an ad that says Campbell just invented a
new-flavor soup, I'll strike. That kind of a day. I'll pipe in
my own secret music that I keep hidden here under my
cortical overlay and I'll free all the Etruscans in all our brains.
Not rock and roll. No, more than that. A blend of Rock and
Mozart and Wagnerian Liebestods and Gregorian chants.
Eskimo folk songs. African. Greek. Hindoo. All bound together by drums that will fascistically force its *way* through
the over*lay* and the country will remember its Etruscan
forebears and begin dancing.

I'll sit in my office turning the level of volume louder and
louder and watch the fires in the distance as men throw in
their attaché cases, their Buicks, their split-level homes and
mortgages and commuter tickets and railroad trains and
husbands and wives and children and bosses and enemies
and friends.

On planes, pilots will race to the sea and passengers will slug
the smiles off stewardesses and stewardesses will pour hot
coffee on all the regular passengers. Bald people—hairless
men, hairless ladies—will whip off their wigs and eyebrows
and grease their skulls and bodies with black car-grease so
the moon will reflect on them when they dance.

Everybody will feel sexy all the time and nobody will mind
what anybody does to anybody else and twins in wombs will
dance so that girl babies will be born with babies within
them and those babies will have babies within them and
within them and within and within.

Buses gallop down Fifth Avenue crammed with naked people beeping the horn, riding on the sidewalk, looting all the
stores, making love in all the churches, knocking noses off
plaster saints, and never getting out of the bus.

They drive the bus down to a subway full of naked dancing people eating pictures of Chinese food off the posters in the subway and the train pulls in and all the naked people push the train off the tracks and leap onto the third rail to see what electricity tastes like.

They race up to Harlem, where naked Negroes have flooded the streets with fat and are chicken-frying Puerto Ricans who cha cha cha and everybody's skin blisters and crackles in cha cha time. The Negroes skewer white people onto maracas and we all dance and devour each other and belch and nobody dies because we've forgotten to and our rib cages become bars of music and our eyes and ears behind the rib cages are notes of music and our spines are staff notes holding us up high and everyone's body is a dance floor and the dancing sets our planet loose and we'll tumble around in galaxies *until,*

in exhaustion, the world will settle back into place and rest and rest and we shall have the beautiful peace of exhaustion.

For that is all peace is—isn't it—exhaustion? The peace of sadness. After copulation all men are sad? And the peace will be sad and slow of breath and even a vague disgust . . .

but there will be exhaustion and yes a contentment and, yes, there shall be peace . . .

I'm going to take the job with Muzeeka, Sally-Jane.

(*He jumps joyously back in bed with his* WIFE.)

(*Blackout*)

Scene Four

"IN WHICH ARGUE MAKES A TERRIBLE DISCOVERY ABOUT HIMSELF."

A blowzy blonde in bed in the lower bunk. Sleepy, drugged. One gorgeous leg hangs over the edge of the bed.

A STAGEHAND *appears at the rear of the stage carrying a brightly painted door.* ARGUE *follows after it. His raincoat and hat are soaking wet. He is nervous, excited, hesitant. He knocks against the door, upstage right.*

ARGUE (*a whisper*): Evelyn Landis? (*No response. The door moves up left. He knocks.*) Miss Evelyn Landis? (*No response. The door moves down left. He knocks.*) Evelyn Landis? (*No response. She stirs. The door moves down center. He knocks.*) Miss Evelyn Landis?

EVELYN LANDIS (*fearful; sudden*): Yes? (*She sits up, groggy.*)

ARGUE: Miss Evelyn Landis?

EVELYN LANDIS (*afraid*): Who is it?

ARGUE: Miss Evelyn Landis?

EVELYN LANDIS (*getting up*): Western Union?

ARGUE: Ahhhh, you're in—

(*She is at the door. She bends down, her hand extended.*)

EVELYN LANDIS: Slip it under the door.

ARGUE (*pause; nervous laughter*): That'd be a trick—a feat of some doing— (*She opens the door a crack. She peeks out. He peeks in.*) I couldn't—ha—slip it under the door. A lovely night out. Hello. Let me dribble off. (*He takes his hat off. The water catches her. She holds her foot against the door so he can't get in.*) It's been raining. Right through to the bone. Have you seen the streets? The colors the neon put in the streets? I thought blood had been spilled in the streets—a massacre all the way up Sixth Avenue. But it's only the traffic lights and when they change the blood turns to green—verdant—green— then the lights burst into these geraniums and the streets have blood again and then green again. Springlike.

(*Her ear is pressed against the door trying to figure out who the hell this is.*)

I saw your ad.

In a men's room in a bar on Greenwich . . . I flushed and saw your name and flushed and blushed, but returned and saw your name and this address and what you did spelled out in a neat, very sincere hand. My wife, Sally-Jane, knows something about handwriting and I've picked up some analysis from her, and we cross our *T*'s—not my wife and I but you and I cross our *T*'s in a way that spells out bizarreness of desire, but a sincerity behind that bizarre . . . it's all there in your *T*'s—in the angle of them over the urinal . . . (*Suddenly embarrassed.*) I hope it's not a joke. Some friend or enemy playing tricks. It's a vicious trick if it's a joke and you should send someone in there with Ivory soap and water and scrub, scrub it off if it's a trick.

(*She signals to a* STAGEHAND, *who enters with a large piece of poster board and a pen. She draws an enormous* T *on the board. It looks like a child's* T, *a Palmer Method* T. *She hands* ARGUE *the board through the narrow crack of the door. He looks at it.*)

ARGUE: That's the *T*! (*The* STAGEHAND *takes the board and exits.*) Yes, I knew there was no joke in your name. Evelyn Landis. Your address. Your phone number. And I was walking thinking of you and what the ad said you did—the graffiti said you did—and watching the traffic lights change the streets from blood to grass and then to blood and then to grass and then I found myself—small miracle—here by your address and a bell by your name. A golden bell with many finger indentations on it . . . (*hesitation*) . . . and I didn't call. I should have . . . (*strong:*) No, I didn't want to and here I am and I wonder if I could come in and you could do to me what the bathroom wall in that bar over on— (*His voice cracks high.*) Do you know the bar? Over on—I'll pay even though it said you did what you did for nothing, but no matter what Chock Full O'Nuts says, there's no law against tipping. Ha? Ha? Yes?

EVELYN LANDIS: No law against tipping.

(*She opens the door. The* STAGEHAND *takes it away.* ARGUE *steps in, remembers to wipe his feet. Takes off his raincoat and shakes the wet off it. A* STAGEHAND *appears as a hatrack.* ARGUE *hangs the coat on it. The* STAGEHAND *exits.* ARGUE *smiles broadly at her.*)

ARGUE: It's not a joke? You do do what the bathroom wall said you did?

(*She instantly transforms into* ARGUE's *idea of the ideal French whore. She poses on the bed and peels off her stockings.*)

EVELYN LANDIS: Ees eet true or not? Zee point ees someJuan said eet. SomeJuan wrote eet. Writing. We mosst trost zee written word. Eef I say Non, eet ees zee lie feelthy, you would feel zee embarrassment. I would feel zee cheepning. You would trost no words for a long time, look on zee written word wiz zee eye yellowed by (*she pulls the stocking off*) Jaundice! (*Soul weary:*) I want you to believe. I want to believe. I want what someJuan has claimed (*the other stocking off*) partout moi to be true. Eef we act out zee lies, make trooth of zee lies everyJuan say partout Nous, zen we would have wage zee major victory on lies, on hate in zee world . . . (*Joan of Arc:*) When a lie becomes truth, eet ees strong. We mosst feed lies ze tiger's milk of truth and in making lies truth we celebrate truth—assassinate BangBang zee lies . . . (*Then, flatly:*) What did they say about me?

ARGUE (*extending a piece of paper*): I wrote out the whole ad— with your address.

(*She takes the paper and reads it a long time. She looks at him. She reads it again. She returns it.*)

EVELYN LANDIS (*very weary*): I better get ready . . . (*She exits.*)

(*He loosens his tie and takes off his shoes and socks. He looks to make sure she's gone. A* STAGEHAND *enters with a telephone.* ARGUE *dials as secretly and quietly as he can. Perhaps the* STAGEHAND *makes dialing noises, then ringing noises.* ARGUE *hushes him.*)

ARGUE (*into the phone*): Maternity ward, please . . . Sixth floor, please . . . (*Urgently:*) This is Mr. Argue. Jack. How is she? . . . Oh God oh God. Is she waiting till the kid is ready for college? . . . Can you look in? Take a peek inside? A boy? A girl? (*The operator is obviously shocked. Placating:*) All right, all right, if she's conscious, tell her I love her. (*Pause.*) I. L. O. V.—Y. That's right, U, and sign it her husband. (*Pause.*) J. A. C. K. That's right. I am at a number where I can be reached. 555-0150. Yes, I'll be here.

(EVELYN LANDIS *reenters carrying a large round heavy flat basket with a hole in the middle of it. Three strands of long strong rope are attached to the basket's rim. The basket is decorated with spangles and streamers and swirls of Day-Glo colors. She plops it down onto the ground. She stares at him.* ARGUE *is embarrassed to be caught with the phone. He holds out the receiver. Laughs nervously.*)

I took the liberty—my wife is in labor. (*He hangs up the phone. The* STAGEHAND *exits.*) Just a local call. St. Vincent's Hospital over on Greenwich . . . They didn't need me. She's been in labor eight hours now. They told me to take a few hours off. Nothing more useless than a father at a delivery. Ha? Even animal fathers go away and hunt till the female has cubbed or foaled or hatched or—well, except the sea horse. He does the birthing himself. (*She sets the basket down. Then he, brightly:*)I—I—I haven't been in the Village in years, since college a few years ago. Am I in Greenwich or East? Which Village is this? I see all you people swarming the streets tonight, you revolters, you rebels with your hair and flowers and beards and birds and braids and boots and beads and I look in your eyes for the visions drugs have given you and tonight I admire you—love you so much. Your free-

dom. Your left-wing connections have covered you with
wings and I want to become—touch some part of—fly up
there with you into the Underground. (*She thinks about that
for a minute.*) Oh, I have my subscription to the *Evergreen
Review,* but I still seem so removed. I live in Greenwich.
Not the Village, but Connecticut. Well, not Greenwich
actually, but right outside—Kennedy, Connecticut—new
development, but nice—and I don't get down to the Village
very much and now, with the baby, I suppose I won't be
getting down here—oh, maybe to see an Off-Broadway
show if it gets good notices— (*No response from her.*) The
Fantasticks. (*Pause.*) I'll have to see that sometime. (*Pause.*) I
suppose it'll be around forever.

EVELYN LANDIS: You don't have to make a good impression on
me. (*She moves to the bed with the basket.*)

ARGUE (*leaning against the post of the bed*): I'm sorry . . . I want to
connect in some way. Tonight I've been remembering a
vision you could call it I had on my honeymoon a few years
ago. I was twenty-two. I'm twenty-eight now, but I could
be thirty-eight or forty-eight or a hundred and eight—and
tonight my wife in pain—Sally-Jane in pain—not needing
me. Feeling violent yes walking down here pressing close to
you all, feeling my own labor pains, my own dreams locked
in by this cortical overlay and maybe my pains are no more
than sympathy pains, but that gives them no less reality, you
know? And you see. I had plans.

(*Muzak plays. A* STAGEHAND *enters right with a sign:* "HE HAD
PLANS." *A* STAGEHAND *enters left with another sign:* "WITH HIS
MUSIC." *The first* STAGEHAND *turns his sign over. It says:* "BUT
ALL HE PLANNED." *The second* STAGEHAND *turns his sign over.
It says:* "TURNED BLAND.")

Bland . . . tonight my cortical overlay weighs down on me
and tonight in that bar I saw your words—well, they're not
exactly Mene Mene Tekel—but my home state gave me my

clue. Connecticut. I want to connect. Therefore, I must cut. Cut off all the ties just for a while, so I can get back to what I was, am, am down deep. Establish my relation to all the Etruscans, all the animals. Except the dolphin, of course. Never the dolphin. Connecticut. Good Christ. Connect? I cut.

EVELYN LANDIS: Boy, are you a sickie.

ARGUE (*threatening*): I am not a sickie. I have not come here for sick reasons.

EVELYN LANDIS (*pause*): I don't want you beating me up.

ARGUE: I am here for political reasons.

EVELYN LANDIS: I just got the bandages taken off from a guy last week—

ARGUE (*cutting her off*): Look, the country is ultimately controlled by the moderates. Right? We therefore need a strong Left as well as a strong Right. Right? Two banks of a river—the Right and the Left—right?—and the river between is the river of moderation that keeps democracy flowing along. Right? I am in that river, but am no part of it and as a consequence am drowning. Right? I want to align myself with you on the Left bank. The Underground. The Left. Right? I can't be a moderate. I don't know enough about either side. But the Right is repulsive to me. I want to stop the war. I love Civil Rights. That leaves only the Left. That's all that's left. Don't you see I'm right? (*He turns to us.*) I can't go back to Connecticut a husband, a father, and that's all. I have to become a citizen. I read *The New York Times* and there's a wall of clay between what's happening in the world and me. Breakthrough. That's all.

EVELYN LANDIS: You want to get this Pledge of Allegiance started?

(*The* STAGEHANDS *enter and help her into the basket and attach it to a hook on the bottom of the upper bunk. On a signal from* EVELYN,

ARGUE *gets into the bunk under the basket. When he is in place, she turns a switch, a gong sounds. Psychedelic lights go on. The* STAGE-HAND *behind* EVELYN *spins her.* ARGUE'*s body pumps slowly.*)

EVELYN LANDIS (*to us*): Look at this phony. He wants some wild psychedelic experience to carry in the wallet of his heart as a secret joy until he's forty when I'll have faded away and he'll have to find another me—maybe a Negress the next time—to get him through till he's fifty or sixty. Some memory to pull out of the wallet of his heart to show in the locker room of his country club, the Yale Club, the club car on the New Haven Railroad so he can feel a regular guy. And he thinks he's having some mystical experience. I'm above him. I can look down into the depths of his fantasy like a witch who reads fortunes in pools of water. He wants his mind to be a Hiroshima of lurid fantasies! Look down! Look down! His skull is a teacup—and the tea leaves of his brain spell out—

ARGUE (*in ecstasies; his body pumping up and down*): It's a nice house. Up to my ass in mortgage. A lawn green as money. At night, a smell of pines. Really. So fresh. Chill. Mist.

EVELYN LANDIS (*to one of the* STAGEHANDS): Could you read us his fantasy? You can't understand one word he's saying.

THE STAGEHAND (*comes downstage to us and reads to us in a flat voice*): A nice house. Up to my ass in mortgage. A lawn green as money. At night, a smell of pines. Really. Chill. Mist. So fresh. Only thirty-five miles out of New York, where my job is. You could be up in the Maine woods or it could be a hundred years ago and I'm a pioneer and the trees are big and the house is big and I feel ownership and I stand in the dark under the trees looking at the frame of yellow light in the darkness—the kitchen light I've left on that frames a portrait of what I am now and always shall be. Sally-Jane calls from the darkness of the bedroom above. "Come up, Come up," and the air is sweet and chill and I go up in the darkness knowing my way up the stairs even though we have lived here only a few months and Sally-Jane is there in bed in a negligee I bought her at Saks to make her look sexy and in this light she is sexy and in the morning the negligee is folded neatly on the needlepoint chair her aunt gave us for a wedding present and we've become one person with many arms and legs and there is the new child folded neatly within her womb and the sun nuzzles our necks like a cat that's been born during the night and I'm up to my ass in debts and I'm still half asleep, yet I smile and say, "Yes, I've done the right thing . . . I love you, Sally-Jane."

(*One of the other* STAGEHANDS *pushes an electric phone ring. It rings and rings.*)

ARGUE (*moaning*): Yes. Yes. I've done the right thing. Yes. Yes. (*Another* STAGEHAND *picks up the phone and hands it to* ARGUE.) Yes. Yes. (*Into the phone:*) This is he. He. He. Has she? It's here? It's here? It's here? It's here? It's here? (*He shudders. His body relaxes. The basket stops spinning slowly.*) I'll be right— yes—over. Yes, right over . . . (*He hangs up the phone. He is exhausted. He smiles up at her.*) I'm a father. I—I'd better go . . . (*He stands up tentatively. He wobbles and smiles. He smooths his hair back. He adjusts his tie. He takes out his wallet. He smiles truly for the first time.*) I'm a father.

(*She holds out her hand. He gives her money.*)

You know what I'm going to do? Knock my wife up again. Her being in St. Vincent's Hospital is the only chance I'll get to come back to the Village and I'll look you up.

EVELYN LANDIS (*taking the money*): You phony.

ARGUE (*putting on his shoes*): No! I'm involved. I have a share of today. I can walk back, splash those colors in the street, pick up my child and say—I don't even know what it is—I forgot to ask—but it's a child and it's alive and I can pick up my child and say, "Your papa has a share of today. Your father is something. Your father dared."

EVELYN LANDIS (*like a Cheshire cat*): You phony. You phony. You phony. You phony. You phony.

(*Pause*)

ARGUE: Now wait a minute. That's one thing I'm—I've got friends here. (*Into the audience:*) We went to school together. We know each other from the club. We ride into New York every day. You know me. I'm no phony. I'm one of you. I've read *Catcher in the Rye.* I know what phonies are. (*He hesitates. Into the audience, a nervous laugh.*) Like Ring Lardner said, You Know Me, Al? (*He looks at us.*) Don't you? Don't you? (*He smiles nervously at us and backs away offstage.*)

(EVELYN LANDIS *climbs out of her basket. She sizes up audience. Bright music plays. The house lights come up full. She runs into the audience, blanketing the audience with cards that read:*)

> EVELYN LANDIS
> 133½ MacDougal Street
> 555-0150
> Chinese Basket Job
> You like?

EVELYN LANDIS (*in the audience; ad lib*):
> Hello, Scarsdale!
> Is that your wife? My lips are sealed.
> Pass the cards down—pass 'em down!
> Give that to your hubby. You come along too. Got something for everybody!
> Hey! There's the bum that gave me the bandages.

(*She hurls piles of cards out. She sings:*)
> Though April showers
> May come your way!

(*She exits at the back of the house.*)

(*House lights down*)

Scene Five

As soon as EVELYN LANDIS *exits at the rear of the house,* ARGUE *comes downstage.*

He starts to talk to us.

His mood is charming and determinedly casual and very embarrassed.

He laughs.

He can't speak.

He smiles.

No words will come out.

He tries to speak.

Two STAGEHANDS *walk behind him with a banner that reads:*

"IN WHICH ARGUE IS AT A LOSS."

They throw it over his head.

(Blackout)

Scene Six

"IN WHICH ARGUE GOES TO WAR."

Indian music plays. Ravi Shankar music.

ARGUE *is dressed in army fatigues. He sits cross-legged in front of the lower bunk and smiles at us. Calmly. Serenely. He might even keep polishing the same spot on his boot over and over again.*

The music stops.

NUMBER TWO *runs in, out of breath. He is approximately* ARGUE's *age and dressed in green fatigues and helmet and is as thick as* ARGUE *is thin. He is as desperate as* ARGUE *is calm.*

NUMBER TWO: Buddy, you got to help me. I been in binds in my life, but, buddy, you're a college man, aren't you? I figure you are—you talk with a nice way and you don't wear any school rings, so it must've been a good school. Guys say they're college men and you look at their ring and it says North Star College in Wyoming or something, but you never say nothing and you talk real nice and you are a college man and I'm in a bind.

ARGUE (*smiling*): I went to Yale and Harvard and Princeton.

NUMBER TWO: Christ. I'm nothin'—Hollywood High—a drop-out—

(*An explosion outside. A* STAGEHAND *comes downstage and bangs two garbage-can lids together.* NUMBER TWO *falls down in fright and huddles close to* ARGUE.)

NUMBER TWO: Buddy, you got to help me.

ARGUE (*amazed*): It sounds so funny to hear my schools out here. Out in a jungle. It doesn't mean anything. It suddenly—no, not suddenly, the last four months, nothing I ever learned means anything . . . (*He turns to* NUMBER TWO *for the first time. Smiles peacefully.*) I don't think I can help you.

NUMBER TWO (*whispering harshly*): What—are you turning snob on a buddy? College guy. You think you're something. We're all in this together. Buddies are to help. Didn't you ever go swimming? The Buddy System. Well, I am holding up my hand because I am drowning.

ARGUE (*pleased*): Ahhhhhhhhhh—

NUMBER TWO (*crawling downstage*): Look out there. Look who's covering the battle tomorrow.

ARGUE: I saw the cameras.

NUMBER TWO: CBS.

ARGUE: I watched the Vietnamese children help drape the cameras in camouflage.

NUMBER TWO: CBS.

ARGUE: Watch them greasing the wheels so the cameras can glide down hills alongside us.

NUMBER TWO: That's it. CBS is covering the battle. I got transferred to this unit two weeks ago when my outfit got wiped out at the Mekong Delta. (*He falls on his back in despair.*) My whole unit was under exclusive contract to NBC. I'm only allowed to fight for NBC. If they see me tomorrow—CBS—they can strip me of all my rank. Cut my payments off back home. They can send me to a unit. (*He sits up.*) Christ, an independent unit. An educational network unit. I'm not fighting for no Channel Thirteen. I don't want to break contracts. I want to kill these VC, but I can't fight tomorrow. You got to help me. You're a college man. Yale, Harvard, Princeton. Christ, you must be about eighty-six years old.

ARGUE: No. No. Twenty-six. Twenty-six!

NUMBER TWO: What the hell were you doing there?

ARGUE (*a frozen smile, reciting*): Princeton to college. Then the Yale School of Music. Then I felt I didn't know anything practical. So off to Harvard Business for a year to learn the rules of the game so I could fit in. I couldn't fit in. I got married. I worked for a year for the Muzeeka Corporation of America. I am drafted. I am happy I am drafted. I looked at my wife and child in Connecticut and thanked Uncle Sam for getting me out of the country, for escaping without the drag of becoming a missing person. I've killed many people in the four months I've been here. I've finally broken through the clay pot that covers my brain. I dance and sing while I shoot and kill. I thank God for war. War is God's invention to make us remember we are animals. Everything is out of my hands . . . I am a little Moses placed in a basket waiting in the bulrushes for my Pharaoh's daughter. I am so happy. Don't you see? Don't you see? Help you? How can I help you? How? How? (*He tries to climb into the upper bunk.*)

(NUMBER TWO *grabs him up and pulls him into the lower bunk.*)

NUMBER TWO: Buddy, calm down. Calm down. Look, lay down. In the bunk. Rest. Rest. You want television on? I'll put it on quiet so the VC don't hear. My old unit wasn't wiped out till the end of *Batman* and *The Ed Sullivan Show*. They must've sat in the black watching for us, watching the television till the show ended and we turned it off. I never knew whether they killed us 'cause we were the enemy or because we turned off Ed Sullivan. (*He rolls a joint and gives it to* ARGUE.) Calm, come on. See, I'm a buddy to you.

ARGUE (*pause; calm*): That's what gets me most. The TV's in the tents. We're here in the jungle and we have television. Tapes of all the Top Ten TV shows broadcast out of Saigon through the jungles—Martha Raye everywhere. I don't like it. It puts sweat in places I never sweat before. Look at my ankles. Soaking wet. Bones weren't meant to sweat, were they? My legs are dry, but my ankles—my ankles—

NUMBER TWO (*rubbing* ARGUE*'s ankles*): Come on—come on— you'll get R&R soon. Go to Hong Kong. Bangkok. Bang a little cock. Thailand. Land a little thigh. That's all you need. Rest. Recreation. Look, I'll tell you what we do. We put on our makeup for tomorrow's battle. We can sleep that much later in the morning.

ARGUE (*sits up, shakily; smiling*): Yes I do want to fight tomorrow. I do want to be in good shape for tomorrow. Yes. Yes. Yes. Killing soothes. Oh, it soothes.

(*They get out their makeup kits from under the bed. They sit side by side on the lower bunk and make themselves up.*)

NUMBER TWO: Don't I recognize you from *Life*?

ARGUE: I was on the cover a month ago.

NUMBER TWO: You sign a contract with them?

ARGUE: No. No. I want to stay independent.

NUMBER TWO: You exclusive with CBS?

ARGUE: We had to. (*Stops. Falls back, laughing.*) The captain's mother lives on a mountaintop in Utah and CBS is the only station she gets.

(*Pause. They make up, getting the eyes and cheeks and chin, with strong harsh lines;* NUMBER TWO *green and black,* ARGUE *red and white.*)

NUMBER TWO: Good thing about NBC—dull days when there's no fighting like Lunar New Year, they rerun our old skirmishes and we get residuals. I see my old buddies and I dream we're all together. Then I watch them get killed all over again and I see me carried off on a stretcher to have my operation photographed for *Saturday Evening Post*. Did you see the spread on me? I love rainy days when we fight only reruns.

ARGUE: CBS doesn't do that.

NUMBER TWO: Shitty outfit.

(ARGUE *is calmed. He looks at* NUMBER TWO.)

ARGUE: Hey, don't make yourself up so well. Do a sloppy job. They know you're new in this outfit and tell them you don't know how to make up for camera yet and they'll stick you in the rear lines out of camera.

NUMBER TWO (*very impressed*): Why didn't I think of that? (*He smears green under his eyes.*) See what a college education does.

ARGUE: No, it doesn't. It doesn't.

NUMBER TWO (*putting black lines in his cheeks*): I been on the cover of *Look* and that spread in *The Saturday Evening Post*. I been in *The New York Times* and the *L.A. Times* and the *Daily News Sunday Coloroto*. (*He shows his face to* ARGUE.)

ARGUE: A little more greenish. They hate you looking sallow. (ARGUE *puts healthy red on his cheeks*.)

NUMBER TWO (*pause*): What do you do back in civvies?

ARGUE: Civvies? I had a job. With the Muzeeka Corporation of America. Piped-in music.

NUMBER TWO: Like my dentist office?

ARGUE: We're everywhere.

NUMBER TWO: No kidding! You arrange all those violins and everything?

ARGUE: Got a degree from Yale School of Music.

NUMBER TWO: That's fantastic that Muzeeka. It deadens the pain and everything. You must've put novocaine out of business.

ARGUE: Yes. That's why I don't think I'm going back.

(*The sudden loud whir of a helicopter booms through the theater.* ARGUE *and* NUMBER TWO *roll off the bunk behind the bunk for safety. Over the whir comes a montage of LBJ's March 31, 1968, speech being broadcast to the troops from the helicopter:*)

"My fellow Americans . . . South Vietnamese govern themselves . . . De-escalate the war . . . Have decided not to seek re-election as President of the United States . . ."

(ARGUE *and* NUMBER TWO *peer up from behind the bunk.*)

"Now, my good soldiers, pray after me . . . Now I lay me down to sleep . . . I pray the Lord . . ."

(*And the machine roars away to other jungles.* NUMBER TWO *has blessed himself and started praying.* ARGUE *is kneeling by* NUMBER TWO.)

ARGUE (*to us*): So it might all be over soon.
I'll believe that when it happens.
It might all be over soon! All possibilities again.
We'll go back home: A new President. A nice President.
Life will be so nice again.

(*Argue's* WIFE *appears in a negligee. She holds out her arms and weeps tears of joy.*)

WIFE: Jack's back! Jack's back! Jack's back!

(*The* STAGEHANDS *appear, one by one, hands extended, big wide smiles.*)

STAGEHANDS: Long time no see.
Long time no see.
You look wonderful.
Isn't that nice.

(*The moment is repeated over and over. "Jack's back—Isn't that nice—you look wonderful—long time no see—"* ARGUE *swings over the bed and comes all smiling down to us as if he's at a friendly interview and answering spot questions from the audience. The voices continue behind him.*)

ARGUE: The killing didn't mean anything. Of course I've killed people. I've put bullets in people's eyes. Thank you! Thank you! I've put let me think bullets in yes people's ears and I've put bullets in . . . thank you very much . . . people's noses and bullets in people's bellies and belly buttons . . . hello there! Sure is good to be back . . . and backs! Yes, people's backs. No, I never used the flames. I never burned anybody. That's one thing. I can wrap my uneaten dinner of course in Saran Wrap—Dow Chemical? Why should it bother me? I never used the flames. Yes, I said people's backs.

(*The handshaking and greetings behind* ARGUE *turn into silence and the gestures turn into stroking.* ARGUE *sits at the edge of the stage.*)

And I'll go back and be convinced, the *Reader's Digest* will convince me, reassure me, and the newspapers and *TV*

Guide and my Muzeeka will stick their hands in my ears and massage my brain and convince me I didn't do anything wrong. And life will be so nice. And my wounds will heal and there won't even be, you won't even see, one little scar, one little belly button, one little memento to show that in violence I was reborn. I'll really miss the killing.

(*The* STAGEHANDS *and Argue's* WIFE *have faded off.* NUMBER TWO *comes down to* ARGUE.)

NUMBER TWO: Hey, Argue, I got an idea. My poppa told me to keep an eye out for a smart guy, a college man, which is why I'm looking at rings all the time, and now that it looks like it's over—peace feelers—take him back home with me. Take him in as a full business partner in my poppa's new business. Fifty-fifty, buddy—right down the line. It's a wonderful town. My poppa's mayor of it all and my ma wins bright blue ribbons from miles around for her beef pot pies and we ride horses and drive cars under oranges that fall from all the palm trees because it *is* country except there's fabulous surf only fifty miles away and the sun always shines except when it's night. *Two* movie theaters. Would you want to come back? Ahhh, you wouldn't be interested. You're an Easterner. Big college man. But my poppa's new business . . . It's gonna be big, Argue. BIG.

ARGUE (*after a pause, comes down to us*): I see what I must do. They tell us—all the sergeants and generals—that we're fighting for democracy. I've never been anywhere near democracy. I meet men from all over America and I realize my America—New York, Boston, Washington, all the towns in between—have nothing to do with America. They're— we're a suburb of Europe. I'll return to the real America, but move to the Midwest, the Far West, the Northwest. It *is* the Buddy System and he has saved my life. I'll divorce Sally-Jane and move out West. Marry a girl from North Dakota. South Dakota. Either Dakota. I don't care. And work with him and forget about changing the world. Work simply.

That's the answer and I won't care about Negroes or Civil Rights or Hippies or Music or the Middle East or lies or the Etruscans or anything because I'll be a member of a small town and live there and that's my whole world.

NUMBER TWO: My company is based on the Roto-Rooter. In Poli, California, where I live now, you can see my sign flashing over the whole San Juarez Valley. The sign's at the top of the San Juarez mountains in high red neon letters—not red red, more like the red in a sunset—more of a pink—my sign flashes and the red glare shines even into Los Angeles if the smog is down: *You Poop It We Scoop It*.

ARGUE: What?

NUMBER TWO: But what we're gonna do—my poppa and me and you—is to move over the whole country with our Roto-Rooter—the same cesspool principle—but hooked up to atomic power. Atomic-powered disposals. Oh, it's wonderful being in cesspools. You lift up the septic tank and look in and know what people have flushed away. Better than reading palms or handwriting analysis, you can tell a person by the secret things they flush away. If we cover cross-country with our Atomic-Powered Sooper Dooper-Pooper Scooper—yes! that's what I'll call it—yes, yes, we can take over the world, the good we can do under ghettos. My dream! Install my SooperDooper under all the places that give America a bad name, that cancel out all the good we're doing here. If there's a riot—trouble—long hot summer, oh God! We pull that chain, our atomic-powered chain and flush away Detroit, Watts, Newark. Flush them away. Clean. Clean. Cool. (*He is beaming.*) And I want you in on it with me, Argue. America: one big cesspool in our hands. You're a smart man and a nice appearance and a pleasant personality and an obvious college education and my wife's got a sister and the four of us—our cesspools powered by the sun—spreading

out from Los Angeles like an inkblot on an enormous
United States–shaped blotter.

ARGUE (*quiet*): Is that it?

NUMBER TWO: Huh?

ARGUE: Is that all we're fighting for?

NUMBER TWO (*stretching blissfully*): That's what I'm scratching
the days off my calendar for.

(*A* STAGEHAND *crosses the stage wearing a sandwich board. It says:*
"GET YOUR HEART IN AMERICA." "HEART" *is not
spelled, but is a picture of a heart. When he turns, the other side says:*
"OR GET YOUR ASS OUT." "ASS" *is a drawing of a donkey.*)

ARGUE (*to us; rueful*): I wish I'd been born a black . . . and when
I got back home, I'd loot all the houses including my own
and march to TV stores and lift open the store window like
a giant Automat and Sally-Jane and I would watch newsreels
of ourselves . . .

And instead I'll go back home and do the only thing I can
do, make my Muzeeka, and we'll be piped into rocket ships
and rocketed from planet to planet, galaxy to galaxy and the
universe will be so nice. So nice. When I go home, I am
what is being looted.

NUMBER TWO (*gets into the lower bunk*): Hey, Argue buddy, tomorrow let's get some special VC and cut off their ears and
we'll get them bronzed and hang them over our desk when
we get back Stateside.

ARGUE (*sitting on the edge of the upper bunk*): Yes. Sure. Good idea.
Yes. (*He reaches to the rear bedpost and takes a machete from it.*)

NUMBER TWO: I'm gonna write a letter to my poppa and my
wife and tell them I found us the brains of our new outfit!
(*He gives the upper bunk a friendly kick. Takes pencil and paper
from under the bed.*)

ARGUE (*to us*): The Etruscans lived and danced about a million years ago and then vanished without a trace like a high curved wave that breaks on the sand and retreats back into the sea. Poof. Vanish. Splash. (*He stabs himself and rolls away with his back to the audience.*)

NUMBER TWO (*overlapping*): "Dear Poppa and Rita Sue . . . wait till you get this news down the old drainpipe."

(*Argue's* WIFE *enters writing a letter and carrying a large baby doll.*)

WIFE: The baby grew another foot today and I've enrolled her in dancing class already and I've enrolled him already in prep school because it can never be too early and I tell the baby every day his daddy is a hero and fighting all those dirty Commies in Vietnam so he can come to us and make more money for us so we can move to a bigger house and go to Yale to college and Europe on vacations and take Mommy to dances and plays and the club. Do you have any friends? Is everybody terribly tacky? Don't worry, your baby loves you and I put the heavy radio on my stomach when it plays Muzeeka and make believe it's the weight of you and then scratch the days off my calendar till you come home to me and the weight is really the weight of you . . . (*She exits.*)

(*Crowds cheer. Drums roll.* EVELYN LANDIS *enters, dressed in an army jumpsuit and green beret. She strips off her jumpsuit and reveals a bikini made of streamers and newspaper columns.*)

EVELYN LANDIS (*to us*): In our heart of hearts, we know God is on our side. I'm an atheist and even I got to admit God is on our side. In America God is on everybody's side! Look at Hubert Humphrey—even he gets around everything.

(*She sings, and with each name, joyously rips a clump of newspaper off herself.*)

Hubert Humphrey
& Jesus Christ
Ronald Reagan
& Jesus Christ
Stokely Carmichael
& Jesus Christ
General Westmoreland
& Jesus Christ

The STAGEHANDS *join in.*

Richard Nixon
& Jesus Christ
LBJ
Was Jesus Christ
Timothy Leary
& Jesus Christ
Bonnie and Clyde
& Jesus Christ
Rocky & Romney
& Jesus Christ
Johnny Carson
& Jesus Christ
Television
& Jesus Christ
Eugene McCarthy
May be Jesus Christ

(*They form a line at the rear of the stage behind the double bunk.*
EVELYN LANDIS *and the* STAGEHANDS *keep clapping in rhythm very
softly.*)

NUMBER TWO (*to* ARGUE): You write that Muzeeka, huh?
You're smart leaving it. It's really dull, you know? But you
know when it's nice? When it's late at night and you got a
bag on and you just got laid and you're driving home over
the Freeway—cars above you, cars below you, lights coming at you—and you got a bag on and you turn on the car
radio and the dream music starts floating in—not making

any point—*not* not funny—not serious—just violins playing
Begin the Beguine–y kind of music, and, late at night, your
car radio starts picking up Oregon and Utah and Nevada and
Canada speaking French. And Kentucky crisscrossing with
Alabama. And that's all your music, huh? Dreamy. You got
to stop and think where you are and you can feel the car
could take right off the road and you pull back the wheel so
it can lift you up and go faster and faster and dawn starts far
away like a pink baby, a pink baby's backside poking up in
the horizon and the air smells clean and it starts to rain and
rain and the music never mounts, never builds, just stays
stardustily in one mood and you love being alive.

(*One of the* STAGEHANDS *uncaps a bottle of catsup and moves behind
the bunk. He pours a blob of it into the white sheet covering* NUMBER
TWO. *The chorus gives a sharp "tip" sound.*)

And it's raining—

(*Another splotch appears on the white sheet. "Tip."*)

And it's raining—

(*More catsup; More "Tip." "Tip." "Tip." "Tip."* NUMBER TWO
sits up.)

Argue?

(*The catsup catches his hand. He looks at the red of the blood.*)

Argue? Argue?

(*Long pause.*)

(*Blackout*)

END

IN FIREWORKS
LIE SECRET CODES

▲ ▲ ▲ ▲

for Adele

IN FIREWORKS LIE SECRET CODES was first presented (as part of its One Act Play Festival) by The Lincoln Center Theater Company at the Mitzi E. Newhouse Theater, in New York City, on March 5, 1981. It was directed by Mr. Guare; the setting was by John Wright Stevens; the costumes were by David Murin; and the lighting was by Marc B. Weiss. The cast was as follows:

#1	William Newman
#2	Kathleen Widdoes
#3	James Woods
#4	Barbara Andres
#5	Graham Beckel

▲   ▲   ▲   ▲

The terrace of a penthouse on the West Side of Manhattan looking over the Hudson River. Night. Fourth of July.

Characters 1, 3, and 5 are men. #3 has a slight English accent. Characters 2 and 4 are women. Everyone is enthralled. Music. [Handel's Royal Fireworks Suite.*] Thunder.*

1: Were you here the tall ships day? Fourth of July, 1976. The Bicentennial. The tall ships sailed up the Hudson. People in New York were happy for a year after that. They had predicted riots and bombings and general terror, but nothing went wrong that day. Right up that river all these tall sailing ships from all over the world sailed. Up. Up. Sometimes even today if I find myself stuck in an elevator or the subway that has broken down and you're there in the pitch black, I'll scream out to the darkness, Remember the day of the tall ships. And one or two people will always scream back *Yes!*

4: Wasn't that a day.

2: Pink. Blue.

1: Pink center! Green. Blue white.

2: Green center. Blue! White! Gold spill!

1: Green blue white.

2: Red blue green.

3: Bougainvillea.

5: Where?

3: The spill.

5: Bougainvillea?

3: Perhaps wisteria.

5: Ahhh. Wisteria.

2: Wisteria?

3: The spill.

2: Ahhh.

3: Gone.

1: Pink white blue. Silver dribble down.

3: Wisteria. Pure and simple.

5: Not bougainvillea.

4: Was it in your lease that Macy's would have to do this in the river right off your terrace?

3: Oh, yes. Right in the lease. Clause 12 triple B. Macy's fireworks right in line with my terrace.

1: Look down below.

5: Right in *our* lease. It's *our* lease, and when the building goes co-op, it'll be *our* bill of sale, *our* deed.

4: I don't want any talk about co-op bargains. Only stories where people are gypped, cheated, or overcharged.

2: Usually they say penthouse, but all they show you are rooms on top of an expensive building with a window box you can barely stand on. But here! This! This—*pent*house! Four sides. You can walk around. You could plant wheat and grow grass. Do they let you bring cows up on the elevator? You could get farm subsidies.

4: Red blue green green.

2: And you must always ask me back here. Not wait for holidays. We could have quilting parties and sewing bees.

5: We could bundle.

2: Yes! Blue blue gold white.

1: Blue blue gold white.

2: We'd have 4-H Club meetings!

4: Red red blue white gold white green.

2: And all the roots from all your crops could travel down all the stories of this building and pass through every apartment and absorb every family up onto this roof in a harvest of urban photosynthesis and these city people will step out of their blossoms and see weather vanes and silos and tractors.

4: Blue red green green gold.

3: You make this simple asphalt roof sound like Kansas.

2: Kansas or Oz. Oz or Kansas. With me, it's always been Kansas or Oz. But here tonight this roof—the eternal dilemma finally and irrevocably resolved. Everything here. I'd never have to leave.

5: But you'd have to.

2: Red blue green. (*Looks at* 3.) Perhaps. Perhaps not.

4: (*To* 1.) I don't like to get too close. Don't lean over!

1: Thousands of people.

4: West Side Highway closed for miles. Don't lean over so!

2: Or did all those people used to be automobiles?

3: Chrysanthemums!

4: Yes!

5: Where? Missed! Damn!

2: Holiday headline: "Frog kisses Buick. Turns it into person."

1: Pink white blue. Sunburst! Dazzle!

4: I feel guilty watching this. I never buy anything at Macy's and here they are, paying for all this.

3: Those ones whistled. Very nice whistle!

4: I *only* go to Bloomingdale's and they never do anything for the city. I've never even stepped foot in Macy's.

2: They *are* the world's largest store.

4: But they seem pathetic. 34th Street. Down there. West side.

3: They *do* do the Thanksgiving Day parade. Miracle on 34th Street. All those great balloons.

4: I know. I know. But I comfort myself this way. I say Macy's does today and Thanksgiving Day; Bloomingdale's does the other 363 days of the year. An interesting person's like a holiday, don't you think? Anytime you see an interesting person on the street, that person is a commando sent out there by Bloomingdale's. Bloomingdale's decorates the streets of New York. Macy's just does windows and two holidays a year. But Bloomingdale's does everything in between. I say to myself that Jacqueline Kennedy would have moved years ago to Greece, but Bloomingdale's signed her to a lifetime contract to stay in New York. And Robert Redford lives in New York on upper Fifth Avenue. Bloomingdale's owns him. And Bloomingdale's brought Nixon here even though he's no holiday. And they do the U.N. and the hostages and the graffiti on the subways. No, Bloomingdale's does lots. Thanks, Macy's, but no thanks. I won't turn on Bloomingdale's. They make every day a holiday.

2: See the last of the sunset over New Jersey.

5: Don't distract us with New Jersey. New Jersey is the worst state in the union. New Jersey blows poison nuclear gases over the river. I wish these fireworks were weapons I could turn back on New Jersey.

2: Everybody has transistors.

5: You need holidays just to stay alive. Just to breathe.

2: Today I can breathe.

4: Don't lean over.

2: What's that playing?

3: *Star Wars.*

2: *Star Wars!* Make it the National Anthem. Take it back— *Rhapsody in Blue!* Make that the National Anthem.

1: Pink green silver!

3: Chrysanthemums again!

4: Yes!

5: Where? Missed! Damn!

3: I was in the South of France one Bastille Day and they had the International Fireworks Exhibition and Red China put on a show in the sky. Chairman Mao instructing the peasants and dreaming of a new world order.

5: All in fireworks?

3: Not like this Macy's rubbish. (*To* 4.) Don't be guilty, dear.

1: Yellow white purple!

4: Don't make me so dissatisfied. I am so satisfied at this moment.

5: (*Imitating* 4.) Don't get so close to the edge.

2: When *I* was a kid, my parents took me to the Christmas show at the Music Hall called *Holiday Inn* and Bing Crosby and

Fred Astaire opened a nightclub that was only opened holidays and Irving Berlin wrote a song for each holiday.

1: White blue blue blue!

2: Bing and Fred fought over the same girl and she'd be in love with either of them on each holiday so there was always suspense.

3: What did they do between holidays?

4: The Music Hall never delved that deep.

2: (*Sings.*) "I'm Dreaming of a White Christmas."

3: That was the Christmas song.

2: I always felt rotten because I had to spend holidays with my family and I could never go to that inn, which was always packed. Holiday Inn. Not the fake one that there's always sixteen miles to the next. No, the real Holiday Inn. In that Music Hall pageant. Blue blue green. (*All sigh.*)

1: The best holiday I ever spent was in Bethlehem. Christmas! I went swimming in the Dead Sea and it's true.

5: What's true?

3: Green gold ahhh.

1: That it's hard to go under. I floated right on top of the water. And that afternoon I went to the camel races in Bethany and I went into a bar and King Hussein was sitting at the bar having a drink with a few people. This will show you how long ago it was. Jerusalem was still in Jordan. And that night we went on a pilgrimage to Bethlehem and went to the Three Wise Men Cafe and the Manger Cafe and the Star Cafe. We brought our own wine because we were travelers, hitchhikers, student wanderers. And the management had us arrested and thrown out because it was their big night to make money, which is one of the things holidays are about. They let us go, the cops, because it was Christmas and we were from all over the world. South Africa. Brazil. We went to the Church of the Nativity and I was up very close for the mass because I didn't want to get claustroid, which I am.

4: Don't lean over!

1: The incense during the mass was very thick and it made me sick. I climbed over the altar rail because it was too mobbed to get out through the church. I didn't want to throw up in the Church of the Nativity. I went backstage of the altar, I don't know what you call it, to get fresh air. A radio crew was there. I said "What's this?" They were from the BBC broadcasting the mass all over the world. "Ahh," I said. I went out through another door where the air was even fresher. The bell tower. An old man was holding on to the ropes. I asked, "Could I help?" He said, "Help? You can do it." The equivalent in Arabic and sign language. The red light went on. The old man signaled me to start pulling the bell. I yanked it down. A loop was on the rope and the old man showed me how to hook my hands into the loop. I began pulling and the bells started ringing, slowly at first, even softly as if I were doing something wrong, but I kept pulling and the bells got louder and wilder and lifted me off the ground. I swung way up in the air and crashed down, way up in the air, crash down. Up. Down! Up. Down. High! Low! High! Low! Twelve minutes. I found out later that the bells rang from the Sanctus to the communion, which is a pretty long time, and I realized, Hey, I am ringing the bells for the midnight mass from Bethlehem and I am being broadcast all over the world. Hello, world! This is me! Parents! Girlfriends! Enemies! Loves! Wives! Ex-wives! Husbands! Ex-husbands! Teachers! Everyone who ever tried to stop me!

4: Don't lean so close!

1: And I went way up, came way down. The old man grabbed
on to my legs to stop the motion of the bells.

3: Pink red orchid!

1: Gradually the bells quieted. Quiet. Quiet.

5: Pink center! Green. Blue white.

2: Green center. Blue! White! Gold spill!

1: Green blue white.

2: Red blue green.

3: Bougainvillea.

5: Where?

3: The spill.

5: Bougainvillea?

3: Perhaps wisteria.

5: Ahhh. Wisteria.

2: Wisteria?

3: The spill.

2: Ahhhh.

3: Gone.

1: Pink white blue. Silver dribble down.

5: Blue green. Pink center.

ALL: Ahhhh.

3: Last May thirtieth—your Memorial Day—I was going over
to Brooklyn to one of your houses.

2: Which of you had a party and didn't invite me? Shame.
Shame.

3: I looked around the subway car and saw a Spanish man reading *El Diario*. A dark Medea of a woman asleep, a Greek newspaper folded over her breasts. I was carrying a week-old copy of the London *Times* so I felt everyone in that car had the correct newspaper. All reading the news of the world in the proper language.

5: Except there was that one man you pointed out. Fantastically unethnic. Blonde. Why was he reading the Manila *Journal?* Urgent headlines: "President Marcos Assaulted." We moved to another car.

3: As I said, we remembered all this because it was Memorial Day. And I was feeling so at home in the world, in that subway. A policeman right by us.

5: And then we heard the scream.

2: Scream?

3: Yes. A scream. Scream for me. (2 *screams.*) Yes. Like that. Only imagine that scream pulled through despair and fear.

2: I did scream with fear and despair. I always scream with fear and despair. Why else would you scream if it weren't with fear and despair?

4: Don't get so close to the edge!

1: Pink! Blue! Look! Look!

3: As I said, imagine that scream with fear and despair and the woman who screamed ran up the subway aisle to the police-man standing by me.

2: What do I say?

3: You say to the policeman, "That man down there, he put his hand on my. On my." And then cry.

2: "That man down there. He put his hand on my. On my," I don't want to make fun of her.

3: Oh, this story makes fun of nobody. You'll see.

5: This story is a photograph. Subway snapshot.

3: Unbeknownst to the woman with the 78 RPM voice, the man who had put his blank on her blank had run out of the car when the subway stopped at Wall Street.

5: The crazed capitalist of Wall Street!

4: Please. The edge. The edge.

3: A Chinese cook gets on at the stop and sits in the crazed capitalist's seat. He opens a Chinese newspaper, all dressed in white, his chef's cap folded out of Chinese newspaper.

5: Fitting in perfectly with our car.

3: The woman drags the copper back as we descend under the river to Brooklyn. She stands in front of her place. "That's him," she says.

2: That's him.

3: The Chinese cook looks up. No English.

5: No English-ee.

3: She begins hitting him. "You touched me," she cries bitterly.

2: I won't do that.

3: You touched me. The Chinese cook holds his Chinese newspaper in defense. Other passengers tell the cop what happened. We speed away under the river from the violation left behind on Wall Street.

5: Where is the crazed capitalist now, I thought! Running up Maiden Lane. Snatching at ladies' parts on Beaver Street. Run! Run!

3: The cop understands what happened. He pulls the lady back to protect the Chinese cook. Everyone begins to laugh.

5: Everyone laughed wildly. It was fantastic to see!

3: Distance under rivers gave us all the terrible objectivity found only in the plays of Molière.

5: The woman began screaming at us all: "Are you all sick? Are you all sick?" But we couldn't help it.

3: Her pain was worthy of the Bacchae out of Aristophanes via Menander passing to Terence.

5: She was in such panic she couldn't hear the explanation that this Chinese man was not the blank who put his blank on her blank.

3: The policeman holds her back. The Chinese cook transforms into Buster Keaton and flees to another car. One of us— Feydeau? Noel Coward? held the door open for a more nimble escape.

5: "Are you all sick?" she cried at us.

3: We come out from under the river, still underground, but at least underearth. We come to the Clark Street stop. "He touched me."

2: He touched me.

3: The cop tried to explain. She'll hear nothing of it. "I don't even want your badge number."

2: I don't even want your badge number.

3: "I don't want anything to do with any of you."

2: I don't want anything to do with any of you.

3: "If this is the human race—"

2: If this is the human race—

3: She won't let anyone speak to her. Give her explanation.

2: Don't speak. No explanation.

3: The doors open. She gets out at Clark Street. We watch her on the platform. She gets back on the train. But moves to other cars. Pushing people out of the way.

5: Just pushing people. Pushing them.

3: People back to the newspapers of their native language. Some people still laughing. Others no longer laughing. But the laughter had purified nothing. Our laughter had only helped anguish move into anecdote. (*Pause.*) Which I give to you right now. (*Pause.*)

2: Pink. Blue.

1: Pink center. Blue. White! Gold spill!

2: Green center. Blue! White! Gold!

1: Green blue white.

2: Red blue blue blue. Green.

3: I've made a great decision. (*Then, to* 2.) Pass the drinks. That's a dear.

2: Down there. What do you suppose all those thousands of people are saying?

4: Don't get too close.

2: I went to New Orleans once and had a city map that showed a street called Mystery Street. I was sure it was an ordinary street but I wanted to see it just the same. I asked the policeman, "How do I get to Mystery Street?" And he said, "You just march up two blocks to Canal Street and you wait for a streetcar marked Desire." The way he said "marked." I always thought Tennessee Williams was a poet. He just wrote down the way people spoke.

5: In England I rode a bus in from Kensington. Two women sat in front of me. I didn't think they were together till one turned to the other and said, "Hilary had another suicide attempt this weekend." The other woman said, "Oh. What did her husband say this time?" The other woman said viciously, "Oh, Hilary's not telling anyone about *this* episode." And they resumed their silent strange ride. I always thought of that bus line as the Harold Pinter bus line. That's all poetry is. Pinter understood the neighborhood on an ordinary day. A day that's not a holiday. The lingo of the streets. The way the rhythm of the town fits on the tongue. On an ordinary day. Not an hysterical day like a holiday. No poetry on holidays. (*A la Pinter.*) Decision? You've made a decision?

1: Pink green. Lavender. Mauve.

5: Blue green. Pink center.

3: I'm leaving America. It's not my holiday. It's not my home. I've lived here twelve years now. I'm not an American. I want to go back to England. The biggest myth in the world is that England and America are alike. We share a language but I don't understand it. I am in the streets and I don't understand what is being said. I want to understand the rhythms in the street. There is a shorthand in the streets. A shorthand in the way people speak. I don't understand America. I don't understand what anyone says. I want to go home and reclaim my language. In fireworks lie secret codes. I've decided it. I'll be back in England by the first of September. I love holidays. I just find it difficult to survive on the days that are not holidays.

1: (*Pause.*) Pink. Green.

2: 1976. The tall ships day. I came here in 1965. My God. I have lived one third of my life in New York. I'm just adding it up. One third. I never meant to stay here. And now it is home. One third. My God.

1: The bells swung up. The bells swung down.

5: You can't leave America. Are you doing April Fool? You
can't leave New York. You know I can't leave. When you
say you're going and announce it like that, I know you're
assuming I am not going with you. I teach. I can't up and
leave. We have put so much work into this apartment. I
can't afford it myself. What am I going to do? I couldn't live
here with anyone else. This is our home. We found this
place. We made it what it is, we made it the showplace it is,
we made it the place where our friends can come and watch
holidays. We had Easter dinner right here on this terrace
even though it was cold. We ate Thanksgiving dinner here
because that was the day we met. I can't up and leave
America. My parents are here. My work is here. My connections are here. I am *from* here. I just can't up and leave.
You can't move away. Make decisions like that and just
announce it.

3: You'll have summer holidays. You can visit me then.

5: It's not the same.

2: And with the budget flights. It's like commuting.

4: Not so close to the edge!

3: I was going to ask you if you wanted to sublet it.

4: Sublet? I can't even look over the side.

1: Stardust. Blue. That's a great one. That's a great one!

3: They're playing *Rhapsody in Blue*.

2: Make that the National Anthem.

4: Red! (*Silence. Dark.*)

1: (*Pause.*) Come on.

3: That's not it?

2: Is it all over?

1: They just stop it?

5: Screw you, Macy's! We want a finale!

4: There we are. (*To* 1.) Pry our car loose from down there. I
   dread the elevator ride down. (*To* 3.) I'm embarrassed to tell
   you. We're moving to New Jersey. A house. Green. New
   Jersey's not really poison. Is it? We're buying. We've
   bought.

2: One third. One third of my life.

1: —Twelve minutes . . . up . . . up . . .

2: And now it's home. Home. (*Pause.*)

3: That fireworks festival in Nice, the Chinese ended with a
   silver vase and then they put gladiola buds in the vase and
   then the gladiolas blossomed and then the petals fell off and
   then the gladiolas withered.

1: All in fireworks?

3: Unforgettable.

1: Where was Chairman Mao?

3: Nothing political. Just beauty.

1: I'll always remember these blues tonight. Every time I see
   wisteria I know I'll think of tonight.

END

THE TALKING DOG

▲ ▲ ▲ ▲

adapted from
A Joke
by Anton Chekhov

CHARACTERS

F	She is in her twenties.
M	He is in his late twenties.
	Each wears a white jumpsuit.
HANG-GLIDER #1	Each of them wears a brightly colored
HANG-GLIDER #2	jumpsuit and black-lensed goggles.

▲　▲　▲　▲

A bare stage. White.

F: Hang-gliding!

M: Hang-gliding.

F: I don't understand anything *about* hang-gliding!

M: You wear this harness—

F: You don't understand—

M: You insert yourself into the machine—

F: I am a complete coward—

M: The wings—the sails—the structure takes care of everything—

F: All I have to do is jump off the mountain. Look at it down
there! It's miles—don't get too close! Watch out for the
edge! Oh dear God, I am not religious and I am praying!
You have me praying! This goddam mountain—

M: This is not a mountain.

F: That's right. Don't pay any attention to my nosebleed or the
thin air or the birds flying below us—the birds have nose-
bleeds!

M: This is the Catskills.

F: The Catskills *are* mountains. The Catskills are not Death Valley turned upside down. The Catskills are not the Gobi
Desert.

M: The Alps are mountains. The Himalayas are mountains.

F: And the Catskills—

M: —are the Catskills. You just strap on your machine and step over the edge.

F: Be careful!

M: Feel the air. The wind. The purity. Breathe deep!

F: And you like to do this?

M: It's what you said about courage.

F: Courage.

M: We have to give ourselves tests of courage all the time to grow, to know we're progressing.

F: Stepping off a mountain is not a progression. Except one way. The air is too thin here. I want to be taken down. By a car. On a road.

M: Don't you want to appear worthwhile to yourself? Don't you want to know you're strong? That you have the strength for life? You have to grow, and the best way to grow—

F: Is not to jump off a mountain—

M: Is by a simple act of courage. And you're protected. You stretch out in the machine. These ropes operate the struts, the wings. You actually control the wind. Mastery over nature! You control the invisible! That which is invisible holds you up. It is impossible to plummet. You are safer in this glider than you are, say, crossing Fifth Avenue. The wind catches you, supports you, welcomes you. A baby could be put in this and glide to earth as safely as Moses drifting in the bulrushes.

F: If I had a baby, I would not let it hang-glide. Moses or not.

M (*sings lightly, seductively*):
> Rockabye baby
> In the treetop
> When the wind blows
> The cradle will rock—

F: The cradle will *drop*. *Drop* rhymes with *top*. Down will come baby, cradle, and all—

M: Just strap the harness on.

(HANG-GLIDER #1 *in his bright-colored jumpsuit comes to* F. HANG-GLIDER *stands waiting, expectantly, good-natured, arms outstretched, welcoming, wearing black-lensed goggles.* F *backs away.* F *looks over the edge.*)

F: I land down there?

M: You land down there.

F: How long?

M: Does it take?

F: How long does it take?

M: It can be over in a few minutes.

F: No!

M: Or if you're good—

F: I want to be good.

M: It can take . . . oh, you can prolong it, prolong the flight, extend the voyage for as long as you can keep control, feel the desire, control the wind, find new bits of current. Slow. Slow. Slow.

F: What's the longest you've ever stayed up?

M: Once—almost an hour.

F: An hour!

M: Generally thirty minutes.

F: You're good.

M: I'm good.

F: Courage.

M: Courage.

F: Were you afraid at first?

M: Everybody is.

F: I want to be strong.

M: Then just do it. You're not alone. Look down there.

F: Other people leaping off the cliffs. Filling the air.

M: This is the hang-gliding capital of the world.

F: I don't see anybody plunging down.

M: They gave you the lesson.

F: We paid the money.

M: I'll fly right beside you.

F: The wind is so high.

M (*testing the wind*): If it wasn't—ahh, then I'd be worried.

F: And you're not frightened.

M: Just that little edge in the stomach—that one frightened edge
    to conquer.

F: We strap ourselves in and go?

M: Yes.

(F *adjusts her harness and stands with her back to* HANG-GLIDER #1.
HANG-GLIDER *attaches her harness to the strap on his chest.* HANG-
GLIDER *lifts her.* F *wraps her legs around* HANG-GLIDER'*s waist and*

extends her arms out in front of her, her back arched, her stomach parallel to the ground.

M *puts on his helmet. He puts her helmet on her head and kisses her hands, which* F *puts into a prayer position.*

HANG-GLIDER #2 *appears in his brightly colored jumpsuit and black goggles.* M *quickly and expertly adjusts his straps onto* HANG-GLIDER*'s chest.* HANG-GLIDER #2 *hikes up* M, *who wraps his legs around* HANG-GLIDER*'s waist, and confidently stretches out his arms, his back arched, his stomach parallel to the ground.*

The HANG-GLIDERS *walk their two passengers to the back of the playing area.* M *and* F *stand side by side.* M *raises his hand.)*

M: Ten.

F: Nine.

M: Eight.

F: Oh dear God.

M: EIGHT.

F: Seven.

M: Six.

F: Five.

M: Four.

F: I can't.

M: FOUR.

F: Three.

M: Two.

F: One.

(And they step forward, their arms extended like wings. The sound of wind. F *screams. They crisscross each other, swooping around the stage, up, down, free. Delight.)*

I'm doing it! I am not believing this! I am doing, actually
doing, look at me doing this! Do you see me?

M: I.
   Love.
   You.

(F *is silent for a moment, not sure of what she's heard. She lifts off her
helmet and cranes her head.* M *signals her wildly to put her helmet back
on, which she does.*
The HANG-GLIDERS *bring them to earth, detaching their harnesses.* M
*rolls and rolls over and over and jumps up vigorously, breathing heavily,
excitedly, pulling off his helmet.* F *is exhausted. She sits in a heap,
strangely troubled.*)

Did—did you like it?

F (*deep breaths*): I've never been more scared—that's a fact. I'm
   shaking. My breath. I'm afraid to feel my pulse.

M: Your pulse is fine.

F: You didn't tell me I'd have to use all my muscles. The power
   in the wind. It's not a free ride. There's no ground below
   you. The psychic shock. I'm in a sweat. The wind is so
   powerful.

M: Did you think you'd just move your pinkie one way and the
   wind does this and you flick your wrist the other and the
   wind does that? All the reading. Lessons. Nothing prepares
   you for the power.

F: Or the sounds.

M: The sounds?

F: I thought I heard something.

M: Heard what?

F: Could—could we try it again?

(SHE *signals. The* HANG-GLIDERS *reappear.*)

M: I thought you didn't like it. The absence of earth. No terra
   firma. Only terror . . .

F: But if you did it with me . . .

(F *looks at* M. *They put on their helmets. Facing each other, they attach
themselves to the* HANG-GLIDERS *once more, and go to the back of the
playing area.
They step forward. They swoop through space. The sound of the wind.
They crisscross back and forth, their arms extended.*)

M: I.
   Love.
   You.

(F *looks up eagerly. They land.* F *rolls over this time more confidently.
She leaps up.*)

F: Again!

M: There's a long line. There's rentals. It's by the hour.

F: Again. Again. Again. Again. Again.

M: There's money.

F: Again.

M: There's time. I have to get back to work.

F: Again.

M: You have to get back to work.

F: When can we do it again?

(F *puts on her helmet.* M *puts on his helmet. They attach themselves to
their* HANG-GLIDERS *and swoop over the stage, whooping joyously.*)

M: I.
   Love.
   You.

(*They land on earth.* F *pulls off her helmet and looks at him expectantly.*)

Yes?

F: Don't you want to say—something?

M: Say something? Like what?

(F *steps back. She studies him.* M *stands there smiling, puzzled. He and* HANG-GLIDER #2 *back away.*)

Like what?

(F *is alone with* HANG-GLIDER #1. *She waits expectantly, checking her watch. She puts on her helmet. She attaches herself to* HANG-GLIDER #1, *goes to the back of the playing area, and steps forward, her arms outstretched in space. She glides.* M *watches secretly, stifling laughter.* F *listens. Silence. She lands.* M *runs out to her.*)

Solo!

F: Where were you?

M: Got stuck in traffic.

F: I waited. Come up with me?

M: I hurt my knee.

F: You didn't hurt your knee.

M: I can't go up. What? Do you think I'm joking? I hurt my knee. The Catskills are the home of the Borscht Belt comedians, but I'm no Catskill comic. I hurt my knee.

F: Are you serious?

M: Of course I'm serious. Why wouldn't I be serious?

F: Do you ever hear voices?

M: Like Joan of Arc? Joan of Arc of the Catskills? Now that's funny.

F: Do you believe Nature ever talks to us?

M: Nature ever talks to us?

F: Nature ever breaks its silence and speaks to us?

M (*stifling laughter*): What does Nature have to say to me?

F: To get us . . . to get us to join her.

M: Her?

F: I don't mean *Her* in a feminist way. I don't mean Her. But I don't really mean *Him*. Nature enlisting us, calling us to join—it's not *It*.

M: Pantheism?

F: Not pantheism because it's not God. I've never used the word *pantheism* in a sentence, so it's a shame it's not the right word, but it's more—

M: Songs like "The Breeze and I"? "I Talk to the Trees"?

F: No . . . maybe yes . . .

M: And what is Nature saying?

F: Don't you know?

M (*stifling laughter*): I just want to get this straight. Are you saying you have heard Nature speaking? This is very fascinating.

F: Have you ever heard it? That's all I'm asking.

M: Are you setting forth a theory or speaking about fact?

F: Could we go up for another ride?

M: My knee.

F: Your knee.

M: I'll hate it when winter comes and the snow and we can't do this.

F: Skiing?

M: Skiing's not the same. Gliding. The air. The height.

F: Just once more?

(*The* HANG-GLIDERS *lift* M *and* F *up and carry them around once more. She listens. He is silent. They land. The* HANG-GLIDERS *retreat.*)

I guess . . . no, just a theory . . . a dopey . . .

M: Oh, theory. I'm not good on theory. I'm a reality kind of guy.

F: Yes. Reality.

M: I had—I don't know what makes me think of this—but I had this friend once who could train animals. She was a great trainer of anything animal. The *National Geographic* offered her lifetime contracts and unlimited expense accounts and introductions to safaris all over the world. And Viola had this Alaskan husky. White. Hairy. Blue glassy eyes of a wolf. And the first time I went to her house to pick her up, I rang the doorbell. The door opens and there is this great Alaskan husky sitting down on its haunches, tail flapping away making this thud thud thud on the hooked rug, and Fido puts up its haunches and says (*Makes a growling noise like a hound baying*):

> I
> Love
> You

F: The husky talked?

M: Viola trained Fido—trained this Alaskan wolf—to turn its growl into this sound:

> Hello
> I
> Love
> You

Well, Viola stepped around the door and flashed a flashbulb taking my photo, the look of shock on my kisser. She loved to take photos of people's faces when they heard this husky talk.

F: Why?

M: A joke. It made her very popular. People would come from various nations to hear the dog talk.

> Hello
>
> I
>
> Love
>
> You

People would swear off alcohol and drugs or else take *up* alcohol and drugs. This dog would look at you with its vaguely Oriental eyes of such intelligence and the growl Hello
You'd think you'd gone over the hill . . . the edge . . . Don't you think that's funny?

F: Well . . . she went to a lot of effort.

M: That was Viola.

F: What happened to Viola?

M: I don't know. The jungles. Talking alligators.

> Hello
>
> I
>
> Lo—

I'm . . . I should tell you. I'm being transferred. Moving to another coast. Well, more towards the middle of the country. But a transfer. You really are terrific, how good you've become. It's really rewarding to see . . . and that sense of courage . . . that . . .

(M *has backed offstage as he talks and is gone.* F *sits by herself, at a loss.* M *appears at the back of the stage, tiptoeing on very quietly. He calls out softly.*)

I

Love

You

(M *stifles a laugh as* F *sits up, listening.*)

I

Love

You

(F *is amazed. She holds her arms out to infinity, smiling. The lights begin to fade on her.* M *comes forward and speaks to us.*)

So I moved away. Transferred to another city, but I always check into New York with the Sunday papers and I saw one Sunday not long ago that she—that she was engaged to some nerd. With a name like Casper. Or Rufus. Some stupid cretinous name. Or else she married him. That page where it's all weddings and engagements and plans for the future. That page. I don't envy Rufus. Or Casper. I mean, she was a—grew into a great hang-glider. Well, an adequate hang-glider, but I don't think she was too much in the sense of humor department. Poor Rufus. Poor Casper. Living with somebody who couldn't take a joke. This is years ago now . . . (*In his dog voice.*)

Hello

I

Love

You

I mean, if I couldn't live with somebody like Viola—well, aside from her dog, Viola had no sense of humor whatso-ever, but aside from that, I'd just as soon live alone as live with somebody who couldn't take a

take a

take a (M *imitates a broken record*)

take a

joke.

NEW YORK ACTOR

▲ ▲ ▲ ▲

NEW YORK ACTOR was first performed at a benefit at the American Repertory Theater in Cambridge, Massachusetts, in April 1992. It was also presented at the New York Public Library for the Performing Arts Reading Room Series on February 1, 1993, under the direction of Neel Keller, with the following cast:

CRAIG	John Vickery
NAT	Stephen Pearlman
EILEEN	Marion Seldes
BARRY	Jerry Stiller
CRITIC	Andre Gregory
CRITIC'S WIFE	Harriet Harris
SAMMY	Barry Sherman
PATRON	Sharon Washington

▲ ▲ ▲ ▲

A theater bar in the west 40s of Manhattan, Joe Allen's to be precise. One wall is lined with brightly colored theater posters of shows with one thing in common.

CRAIG, NAT, BARRY, *and* EILEEN *sit at a table.*

CRAIG: To see these posters. I know I'm back in New York. (CRAIG *raises his glass to the wall in question.*) To you, "Rachel Lily Rosenbloom."

NAT: Cheers, "Mata Hari."

BARRY: Hail, "Fig Leaves Are Falling."

EILEEN: Hey, "Dude!"

CRAIG: "Here's Where I Belong!"

NAT: "Come Summer!"

BARRY: "Hot September!"

EILEEN: I still remember you, "Carrie!"

CRAIG: "Breakfast at Tiffany's."

NAT: Arriverderci "Via Galactica!"

CRAIG: "I'm Solomon!"

EILEEN: The disaster wall. Hail to you shows that ran only one performance.

CRAIG: Yes! Flaunt your failure so it can't hurt you! Oh Christ it's good to be back in New York!

(BARRY *looks up at the TV screen.*)

BARRY: Here it is! Here it is!

EILEEN: Yes! Quiet! Omigod!

(*They all look up.* EILEEN *and* BARRY *recite along with their TV voices.*)

EILEEN'S VOICE: Why would our old cereal want us to get cancer?

BARRY AND EILEEN (*together*): NU-TRIX Bran wants us to live a long long time.

(*They watch in silence for five seconds and then the commercial is over. Everyone applauds.*)

CRAIG: You were great!

NAT: You'll save lives!

EILEEN: You looked like a bank president.

BARRY: Very Katharine Hepburn you.

EILEEN: I hope we work together again.

NAT: This is going to go national.

CRAIG: You'll make a lot of money.

EILEEN: Don't you have a commercial coming up?

NAT: Athlete's foot. The third toe. But it can't all be *The Oresteia*.

EILEEN: Did you see the Peter Brook?

NAT: Out in Brooklyn? So so. (*To* CRAIG:) But here's to you. To be on Broadway!

BARRY: Your series finally over!

NAT: I liked "Lawyer from Another Planet."

CRAIG: Indentured slavery. Five years of torture.

EILEEN: I've never been to California.

NAT: But it gave you recognizability.

BARRY: Plus cash. And those residuals.

CRAIG: We *were* like a family. Our own repertory company. For a while. But still—

EILEEN: But "The Locksmith." To be in the play of the year. Everyone on tenterhooks!

BARRY: You open in a month?

NAT: I've got *my* tickets. I'm a Tony voter.

BARRY: No disaster wall for you.

EILEEN: Not after two years in London.

NAT: They'll give you respect.

BARRY: But no residuals.

CRAIG: Katinka and I let our place go in L.A. Half an acre in Studio City. Took an apartment here. Talk about "Little Shop of Horrors." The kids didn't want to move east but I said, Look! your father is back being the greatest thing anyone can be—a New York actor. The British director's crazy about us. Says the American cast has an energy the English lack. Although I'm not crazy about some of the cast.

BARRY: Who are you? I saw it in London.

CRAIG: The Locksmith.

BARRY: The Locksmith! The guy in London won a prize.

NAT: The Oliver!

BARRY: You got the Locksmith!

CRAIG: They called me. I read. I got it. Simple.

NAT: You went to London?

CRAIG: They came to L.A.

NAT: They skipped New York? Fuck 'em. Although I'm glad for you.

EILEEN: I've never been to London. Always afraid to leave New York. Always afraid the big call would come and I'd miss it.

BARRY: Well, this bran flakes will give you financial freedom.

EILEEN: And residuals.

CRAIG: It's like what Laurence Olivier said. "If acting decides to embrace you and take you to its heart, it will hurl you up there among the gods. It will change your wooden clogs overnight and replace them with glass slippers." I'm not saying I'm Sir Larry—

EILEEN and BARRY: No no no—

CRAIG: but I'm thrilled to be back in New York. Out there I was ready to kill myself.

NAT: Kill yourself?

CRAIG: Terminal likability. Any time you read a freeway fatality, know it's an L.A. actor who crashed his Volvo into an overpass, sick of being likable. That's . . . that's what happened to me.

EILEEN: No!

CRAIG: I tried to crash my new Volvo into a rail guard. I pulled over to the side of the road. Asthmatic. Sweating. Freezing. My series was cancelled. I took it as a sign. I knew I had to get out.

EILEEN: I'm so glad you're back.

NAT: Bravo.

BARRY: I was up for a Volvo commercial. Voice over.

CRAIG: The difference between being an L.A. actor and a New York actor is in L.A. you don't ever dare be tuned out of somebody's living room. Never be unpleasant or complicated. But a New York actor is fearsome. A New York actor changes his soul. A New York actor has a soul to change. Christ, listen to me. I'm alive! Being what God meant me to be!

NAT: That's why I could never make it out there. I'm not likable. I like that about me.

CRAIG: An L.A. actor has to make Jack the Ripper likable.

BARRY: Charlie Manson a sweetheart—

NAT: Richard Nixon a heartbreaker—

CRAIG: Although I got offered an interesting part wouldn't you know the day before I left. Richard Nixon's hairdresser. True story. Haircuts he gave during crises.

BARRY: Vietnam?

NAT: Watergate?

CRAIG: Snip snip snip. Very moving.

BARRY: You don't think of Richard Nixon having haircuts.

NAT: I suppose he must have.

BARRY: Richard Nixon with his hair down to his shoulders.

NAT: Richard Nixon with a ponytail.

EILEEN: Nixon in a beehive. I like it. But you turned it down.

CRAIG: because I'm the greatest thing there can be

NAT: New York actor!

CRAIG: A killer! A giant! A teller of truths! Brando! Monty Clift.

EILEEN: George Scott.

BARRY: Jimmy Dean.

NAT: Jason.

BARRY: Eli.

EILEEN: Rip.

CRAIG: New York actors. They played Broadway. I'll tell you a secret. It's driven me crazy all these years. (*Draws chair closer.*) I never played Broadway.

NAT and BARRY and EILEEN: What? No? Really?

CRAIG: I'd wake up in the middle of the night and say my life is worthless because I never played Broadway. And then along came the Locksmith. Another round? My treat.

BARRY: There's life beyond Broadway. You ever played Seattle Rep? You ever played Yale Rep? Hartford? The Arena?

CRAIG: Readings at the Taper. I kept my hand in.

EILEEN: Seattle Rep. The Goodman. Trinity Square.

BARRY: Williamstown. New Jersey Shakespeare. ART.

NAT: That's our national theater. Broadway's a dream for you but it's not for me. Shakespeare in the Park. I won an Obie.

BARRY: An ensemble Obie. The whole cast got the Obie.

NAT: You ever even been suggested for anything resembling an Obie?

(CRITIC *and* CRITIC'S WIFE *sit at the next table and pick up menus.*)

EILEEN (*sotto voce*): See who's at next table? The new guy at the *Times.*

NAT: The new guy?

EILEEN: They're going to have a Tuesday lynching party. A reviewer reviews the reviews. That's him. That's Tuesday. Don't look.

BARRY: What the world needs now. More reviews. Don't look.

NAT: Well, this guy loves me. You read my reviews on *Tomorrow's Meadow?* A love letter from him.

EILEEN: That's six years ago in a small weekly magazine.

CRAIG: So what! Today he's the *Times*. Tell him—

NAT: Tell him what?

CRAIG: Thank him for your review. Someone who appreciates your craft. God, we're all in this together! The Theater! This endangered medium! A precious craft like lace weaving! Essential to our souls like water. He wrote about you? Thank him for what he wrote. Appreciate appreciation. Stick up for yourself! You're a New York Actor.

(NAT *pauses and then gets up and stands over the table until the* CRITIC *looks up.*)

CRITIC: I'll have the black bean soup.

CRITIC'S WIFE: No, dear. You have an opening tonight. Try the consommé.

NAT: I'm Nat Boyle.

CRITIC: Yes—and the La Scala salad.

NAT: "Tomorrow's Meadow"?

CRITIC: Is that a horse?

NAT: A play. (CRITIC *and* CRITIC'S WIFE *laugh.*) I was in it.

CRITIC'S WIFE: We have a curtain—

CRITIC: Can we order?

NAT: Sir, you wrote this review of me—

CRITIC'S WIFE: You cannot hold him responsible—

(NAT *takes out a clipping from his wallet.*)

NAT: You said I was "almost perfect." I had you laminated.

CRITIC: *Tomorrow's Meadow?*

NAT: I just heard your good news and wanted to tell you it's great news for the theater community having more reviews and how everyone admires you and what an addition and privilege you are. Your judgments are synonyms for perspicacity and insight into the craft of where we theater artists are striving and it's a great day for the New York theater and I speak for all of us personally looking forward to reading you and if you some Tuesday find yourself writing a column about "Down Memory Lane," about performances you've admired over the recent years—Nat Boyle! Meeting you. It's a privilege. And let me order you a waiter! Waiter! Pronto!

(NAT *returns to his table.*)

NAT: Oh Christ, was I an ass kisser?

BARRY: Oh no! A blow job doesn't make you an ass kisser.

CRAIG: Bravo! Bravo!

(SAMMY *enters, sits down.*)

SAMMY: Congratulate me! I just came from a great audition! I think I got the part! This new English play! They're replacing the guy who's doing the Locksmith. Some L.A. actor. Where's a waiter! I am thirsty! I auditioned my heart out! I sang! I swear to you I sang! Waiter! A bottle of champagne! No, the Krug—

(CRITIC'S WIFE *looks for something.*)

CRITIC'S WIFE: It was right here. It was right here.

CRAIG: One moment. One fucking moment.

(*The* CRITIC *taps* CRAIG *on the shoulder.*)

CRITIC: Did either of you gentlemen see my wife's purse?

CRITIC'S WIFE: It was right here. It was right here.

CRAIG: Shut up, asshole, I'm talking!

BARRY: Shut up! That's *The New York Times* Tuesday.

CRITIC'S WIFE: I hung my purse over the chair.

CRAIG (*to* SAMMY): What is this? April fools?

(BARRY *whispers to* SAMMY.)

SAMMY: What did you say?

(BARRY *whispers to* SAMMY, *now audibly.*)

BARRY: Locksmith. Him.

SAMMY: What did you say?

(CRAIG *stares at* SAMMY.)

CRITIC'S WIFE: It was right here. It was right here.

SAMMY (*to* CRAIG): Oh fuck. I'm really sorry.

CRITIC (*to* NAT): Could we have it back?

NAT (*to* CRITIC): What are you looking at me for?

CRITIC'S WIFE: I had it. And then you leaned over. *Tomorrow's Meadow.*

BARRY: Cover your face.

EILEEN: Move to another table!

(EILEEN *and* BARRY *move away, napkins over their faces.*)

CRITIC: You leaned over my wife.

NAT: To talk to you. To talk you got to lean.

CRITIC'S WIFE: I hung my purse over the chair.

CRAIG: What are you saying you got a part?

SAMMY: It was only sort of definite. Look—don't take it personal.

CRAIG: Who's got a quarter?

SAMMY: Here's a quarter.

CRAIG: I don't want a quarter from you.

(CRAIG *runs off*.)

SAMMY: Be happy for me.

(SAMMY *runs off after* CRAIG. *The* CRITIC'S WIFE *is down on all fours looking under the table.*)

CRITIC'S WIFE: It had everything in it. Keys. Money.

(NAT *gets down on the floor.*)

NAT: Why would I take anything from you?

CRITIC: Because you're sick! Now I'm in a foul mood and I have to view a play I don't want to see anyway. Wait! I remember you! Nat Boyle! That's your name!

NAT: No! Not Nat Boyle. Pat Doyle. Doyle! That's my name. You need money? Here—take mine? You want eyeglasses? A wallet?

(NAT *empties his pockets.* CRAIG *returns,* SAMMY *following.*)

CRAIG: There's a message on my machine to call the producers.

SAMMY: Maybe they want me for understudy. Maybe it's for the tour.

CRAIG: I can't go back to L.A. But how will I stay here in New York? Out there I tried to kill myself. Maybe that's the answer. Why not! Why not!

(CRAIG *runs out of the theater bar.*)

SAMMY: Come back!

(SAMMY *follows. The* CRITIC'S WIFE *holds* NAT *by the leg.*)

CRITIC'S WIFE: Thief! Thief!

(*The* CRITIC *pulls his* WIFE *away.*)

CRITIC: Sweetheart! Quiet! I don't want my name in the paper!

NAT: Oh but you can put my name in the paper! "Almost perfect" yesterday. Thief today!

(NAT *punches the* CRITIC. *The* CRITIC's WIFE *punches* NAT.)

CRITIC'S WIFE: Thief! Thief!

(*They fall off, fighting.* EILEEN *and* BARRY *reappear, very excited.*)

BARRY: Here it is again!

EILEEN: Everyone! Quiet!

(EILEEN *and* BARRY *look up as before. They recite along with their voices.*

EILEEN/WIFE: Why would our old cereal want us to get cancer?

BARRY/HUSBAND: Let's be grateful NU-TRIX wants us to live a long long time.

(*The commercial is over.*)

BARRY: You gave me so much.

EILEEN: You gave *me* so much.

(*Two* OUT OF TOWNERS *sit at the vacated table and look around, thrilled.*)

OUT OF TOWNERS: *Rachel Lily Rosenbloom!*
  Mata Hari!
  La Strada!
  Fig Leaves Are Falling!
  Dude!
  Home Sweet Homer!
  PrettyBelle!
  Come Summer!
  Breakfast at Tiffany's!
  Carrie!
  This place is adorable!

(*Blackout.*)

END